the complete guide to London's

Antique Street Markets

Jeremy Cooper

the complete guide to London's Antique Street Markets

with 70 photographs and 10 maps

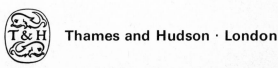 Thames and Hudson · London

To Helen

© 1974 JEREMY COOPER

Printed and bound in Great Britain by Jarrold and Sons Ltd, Norwich

ISBN 0 500 01115 x hardcover
ISBN 0 500 27046 5 paperback

Contents

THE MAPS

Acknowledgments

In writing a book about the antique street markets of London an author's principal debt must necessarily be to the people of the markets themselves. In a sense it is their book and not mine. All the markets discussed in these pages have, over the years, given great pleasure to thousands of regulars and to millions of casual visitors, and this book sets out to describe the people and the places responsible for this considerable achievement. If, by errors or omissions, or by contentious statements of opinion, any of these market people find cause to be annoyed, it will be to the author's grave regret.

Many friends and acquaintances in the market have helped directly with information and suggestions; many more have been equally helpful in less direct ways. While thanking Mr John Friend and Mr Bill Jones by name, I would like to express my gratitude to everyone else as well.

The photographs have turned out to be an integral part of the book, and in this I was extremely fortunate in being introduced by the publishers to Harold Chapman, who has captured the human qualities of the markets with remarkable precision. With the exception of plates 33 and 41, which are by courtesy of the Newcastle Museum, all the photographs of objects illustrating Part Two are from Sotheby's Belgravia, and were taken with customary excellence by Jeanette Kynch.

J.C.

How to use this book

The main text (Part One, pages 11–77) needs no explanation. The first three chapters each describe the character and qualities of one of the major London street markets specializing in antiques, while chapters four and five deal more briefly with the East End and smaller markets.

Readers interested in starting a new collection will find in Part Two (pages 78–111) a general introduction, and a discussion of thirty subjects (arranged alphabetically) that are worth attention on the market stalls. In each case price levels are indicated, and accessible further reading is suggested wherever possible.
These first two sections are intended to entertain general readers and at the same time help prospective market visitors to get the best from the markets.

Market visitors will find their **practical queries answered** in Part Three (pages 112–43), which is a direct guide. The markets are treated in order of their size and importance for antiques. For ease of reference, the same questions are dealt with in the same order in each chapter:
A. when the market is open
B. what is sold there and the general level of prices
C. how to get there
D. local food, drink and entertainment
E. where specialist shops and stalls are to be found (stalls and shops are listed under alphabetical speciality-headings for Portobello Road and Camden Passage; map references are given in addition to addresses)
F. for prospective stallholders, how to obtain a stall

The Maps should be used in conjunction with the guide (above). For each market the first map marks the general area, buses and Underground stations (compare section C above). Following maps show the area in detail and, in the case of the larger markets, pinpoint different kinds of specialist shops and stalls by means of a key (compare section E above).

NOTE Only shopkeepers and stallholders who have already proved their intended permanence have been listed under specialities and included on the maps. Nevertheless, change is inseparable from a living market, and readers in the years to come must bear in mind the advisability of checking for themselves on the times and habits described in the guide.

Prices indicated in Part Two are correct at Spring 1974, but should be checked and updated as necessary periodically thereafter.

However, the description of the qualities of the markets, in Part One, will, the author hopes and believes, long remain true.

Not a tourist in sight before 9 o'clock on the Portobello as rival dealers wander up and down taking the pickings from the jumble of half-opened cardboard boxes and bags

Part One: Introduction to the Markets

1 The Portobello Road

Saturday on the Portobello

Every Saturday morning in all weathers the long, winding Portobello Road on Notting Hill attracts thousands of stalls and street-sellers to form one of the biggest and most colourful street markets in all Europe.

Returning home in the early hours of Saturday morning, a Portobello local sees no sign of market life in the shanty town atmosphere of slightly crooked terrace-houses receding down the hill towards North Kensington Then gradually, almost stealthily, motor-cars creep round dark corners and draw in at vantage points by the side of the curb, until by 6.15 the road will be half-full of parked cars. Still the Portobello maintains an eerie silence, and the macabre, open-mouthed poses of drivers sleeping at the wheel send shivers down the spine. Something is happening but one cannot be sure exactly what, particularly when two suntanned Texan ladies approach from the direction of Notting Hill, angel-like in their fluorescent rainproofs.

But it definitely is market day, and the appearance of these first potential customers stirs the sleeping stallholders into action; a regular politely explains to the puzzled Texans that it all starts rather later in Portobello than Bermondsey. However, these ladies need not regret their early arrival, for between the hours of 7 and 10, before the arrival of the milling crowds, the Portobello Market has a special flavour that can never be tasted during the rest of the busy day. During these early hours the market belongs to the people of Portobello, to the stallholders and to the regular buyers whose whole week is directed to the Saturday climax of the market.

At about 7 o'clock shapes begin to emerge from the shadows, and stallholders start to transfer their baggage from the loaded cars to the pavement and then to the stall. Dan, whose tattooed frame is recorded in numberless tourists' photograph albums, is always one of the first arrivals, and his battered van gives birth to a startling litter of plastic laundry baskets in pastel shades. Other stallholders patiently await the opening of the arcades and the arrival of the Borough lorry carrying street stalls. A mood of hungry tension pervades that part of the market as dealers knock impatiently at the door of the café Casa Maria, whose drawn blinds conceal all signs of life despite the tantalizing smell of fried sausages and bacon. Further down the hill, Harris's Arcade is normally the first to raise its shutters, and inside an old lady sits reading a paper beside her fully-lit stall; she might never have moved since last week but for the paper being today's. The busiest spot at this time is the butcher's shop, where gaping carcasses of meat are hustled about the racks in preparation for the hectic Saturday trade.

Near the top of the hill someone turns a Caruso cylinder on his phonograph, and the 'Good Fairy' arrives to transform a pub's backyard into a popular boutique of Superman sweat shirts, denim jeans and army surplus uniforms. The young men who run the Good Fairy are masterly in their handling of the tall tarpaulin tent, and in no time their bower is festooned with colourful clothes. To the dealer passing by Graham Webb's window, the can-can girl automaton, throwing up her skirts to reveal the skeletal mechanics of her thighs, begins to look less disturbing in the brightening light of day.

As the road comes to life an outsider might feel that nothing much goes on apart from the erecting of stalls and the casual unpacking of goods. The careful observer will see that in reality many dealers do more business in these early hours on the Portobello than in the whole of the week before. In contrast to the crush of midday this early dealing is certainly quiet and calm, but there is a controlled excitement and subtle intimacy in the air.

This is the time when experience of the market must be put to good effect, for the fierce competition between rival experts ensures that only the first arrivals at a newly unpacked stall can hope for a real discovery. Regulars get to know the habits of their favourite stallholders, and pace up and down the road waiting to dart in and capture that vital moment when the boxes and packages are opened to buyers. The action always remains quiet and controlled however large the crowd gathered round a tiny stall. No one would think of offering a price for an object once it is in another dealer's hand, and, knowing his clients as well as they know him, a stallholder carefully offers each object to a specialist dealer or collector in that particular field. Years of dealing together have even removed the necessity for money to change hands immediately; a price will be mentioned, the vase or snuff-box is turned over in the hands once more, and with a nod and a smile, the purchase is hidden under the counter to await payment and collection later in the day. There are no rituals, no rules, no preference given to the scores of West End dealers standing with the rest, but business is conducted with a sureness and confidence only possible among true professionals.

No one can deny that the antique trade has its shady side, but at 9 o'clock on a sunny Saturday morning in the Portobello, nothing seems more charming and satisfying than the life of an antique dealer. The sense of comradeship is so real that one can almost feel it physically, as when a rich and established silver dealer stops suddenly in his tracks to chat with an old lady who ceased years ago to handle anything of interest to him, but who remains important because she is a Portobello friend.

The intense rivalry which is also part of Portobello dealing comes into the open at 8.30 precisely every Saturday morning when a positive scrum forms outside Collectors Corner waiting for its appointed opening. Of the twelve dealers inside preparing for the onslaught at least half have a reputation for bringing new goods to the market every week, and the tension that builds up outside quite contradicts the normal gentlemanly spirit of the market. It is especially amusing to watch if the week before a remarkable find has been made. The bright red doors swing open, caps and pipes are knocked flying into the air, shins are bruised as a tide of dealers jostles competitively about the stalls; as often as not there will be absolutely nothing of interest the second week, and puzzled optimists shuffle in and out of the door for the next twenty minutes, refusing to believe that the nest is empty.

Finally, with a last look to see if some missing stallholder has eventually turned up, the dealers wander off for a well-earned breakfast and leave the market to the crowds who bring new moods to the Portobello.

From the Tube most visitors will walk to the market, unless a 52 bus happens to round the corner at the right moment. It is always worth dropping into Carriés at No. 32 Pembridge Road on the way, for the massed shelves of Staffordshire figures, dolls, postcards and other colourful Victoriana provide an appetizer for the market to follow. Apart from Geoffrey Van's minerals and Shirley Hirst's period furniture, the first stretch of the Portobello is interesting only for the recently renovated artisans' dwellings on the right, probably among the first houses to be built on the Portobello Road in the 1860s, before which it had been a pleasant country lane leading to Portobello Farm, so named in 1740 to commemorate Admiral Vernon's famous victory at Puerto Bello in the Gulf of Mexico. The Late Victorian market here was by all accounts an extremely lively place, with the 'costermongers' (fruiterers) attracting the crowds, and the crowds attracting a host of conjurers, flame-eaters and other street performers. Later, immediately before and after the war, the Portobello Market lost its good reputation and the whole area became known for racial violence and prostitution rather than antiques. This will be hotly denied by many of the old families who still trade on the road; while admitting that the Portobello only became well known for antiques in the late 1950s, these old inhabitants claim to have done flourishing business 'in the trade' all their lives. The truth is that only in the last fifteen years has there been much money to be made in second-hand furniture and Victoriana, and the Portobello Market has grown in size and reputation concurrently with the post-war boom.

Nowadays the market begins at the crossing with Chepstow Villas, and visitors immediately notice the picturesque pink-painted Centaur Gallery, the imperial red, white and blue of Georgian House, and the elaborate illusionistic name-board hanging outside 'Alice's' crowded shop. On the other side of the street Lord Bangor's 'Trad' epitomizes the boundless variety of Portobello taste, with its gaudily-painted carousel animals sharing the window with brass portholes and binnacles rescued from the ship-breaker's yard. From this vantage point at the top of the hill the crowded street winds away into the distance, an amazing medley of races, creeds, colours and characters. It is amusement enough to spend an afternoon just watching the antics of the crowd.

Few tourists can resist stopping at the first line of stalls at the top of the road. Outside the Georgian House a gigantic twenties gramophone horn throws forth muted sounds of Glenn Miller and the big bands, while four ancient Belgian 'grandes dames' hobble about taking photographs of each other by one of the Union Jacks that always hang there. In front of Alice's window a long stall is piled high with gas-masks, army berets and flying helmets that delight a coach-load of German youths, while at a near-by stall a flourishing trade goes on each week in floppy felt hats and tartan berets. The voluble stallholder can hardly keep a straight face as he per-suades an old French priest that the bobbled beret perched on the top of his head looks 'Paris chic'. Everywhere colourful characters sell assorted fineries and paraphernalia, and newcomers must look about carefully to avoid missing interesting smaller establishments like the Portobello Mews Market in Denbigh Close.

The halfway point of the antique market complex is at the Westbourne Grove crossroads, and most of the large indoor markets are in the lower section; ten years ago, when the market was half the size and five times quieter, stallholders at the top of the hill kept an eagle eye trained on the lower road, and the moment a stall was vacated they would gather every-thing up in a blanket and run down the road to claim the better pitch. In this block between Westbourne Grove and Colville Terrace the sale of antiques from stalls is still livelier than anywhere else. Near the top a sharp silver dealer has exchanged the Council's canvas roof for a perspex cover-ing, and his silver stands out like a beacon beside Dan's stall of tangled bric-a-brac.

But even Dan's striking face and interesting oddments fail to distract a perspiring American from his determination to track down the source of the delicious ice-creams that have suddenly appeared in people's hands. Eventually he finds the ice-cream and Coca-Cola booth outside the bakery, and a contented smile creeps on to his round face. His partner calls in vain for him to inspect yet another 'cute' silver-plated snuffer.

Just by Vernon's Yard there is a break in the steady flow of human traffic through the market as passers-by suddenly find ridiculously-clothed monkeys being thrust into their arms by a band of photographers. Sometimes the scene becomes quite disagreeable as frightened foreign visitors struggle to free themselves from the clinging animals, while the photographers push them into position for a quick snap. The whole operation is most uncharacteristic of the Portobello, which prides itself on the unforced freedom of the market and is served so much better by the talented street musicians and entertaining buskers and beggars who are described in a later section of this chapter.

In memory the Portobello is always bathed in bright sunlight, as collectors sit sipping coffee on that convenient flat roof to the Corner Antique Market overlooking the busy street-scene. But when it rains in the Portobello, just like everywhere else, instead of sinking into a bad-tempered sulk the market assumes a kind of mad gaiety. Bad weather keeps few stallholders away, and once having made the effort to come, most are determined to make the best of things. With typically English phlegm a regular adroitly manœuvres his pots and vases to catch the drips from a leaking roof, and continues his perusal of a new book on pottery marks.

After a few minutes' heavy rain a cascade of water shoots down the hill threatening destruction to any carelessly placed packing-box, but nothing seems to alter the contented smiles of the stallholders. As soon as rain starts, the large indoor markets like Hildreth's Portobello Antique Arcade and the Red Lion become packed with dripping bodies. A whole new vista opens up inside, and the official figure of nearly two-and-a-half-thousand Portobello antique traders begins to seem feasible. Some of the new arcades on Westbourne Grove have been fitted with tiny cubby-holes crushed together with room for little more than a cramped stall-holder, but on the expansive floor of Hildreth's the tables are set out with a broad display of varied delights.

Beyond Lonsdale Road, fruit stalls become intermingled with the antiques, and the busy scene of the food market suddenly comes into view. 'Cosebelle' in Portwine's Arcade sends collectors on their way with the notice 'Do not put the hand in – eh! eh! eh!', and across the road a rusty cannon-ball is proclaimed the 'Last shot fired at Waterloo. Not for Sale.' Across the threshold of the lower market stands a beaming, bearded hippie, dressed in a dashing outfit of coloured patchwork suede and bearing placards demanding freedom for cannabis. Two worlds meet as a pious man from the 'godsquad' with his 'Jesus Saves' leaflets finds no answer to the commune's invitation to a free festival of Love, Peace and Freedom.

Tourists and collectors in the mid-morning crowds on the Portobello

There can be no doubt that the comparatively unspoiled charm of the antique market survives largely through the protection of the fruit and vegetable market; for at the crossing of Colville Terrace the traditional 'coster-mongers' scene flows directly on from the antique stalls without the slight-est break in the passage of the crowd up and down the road. Rosy has kept a barrow there at the crossroads for decades, and with a glass of Guinness tucked among the herbs she keeps a daily watch on the life of both markets. Ever since the Portobello was first developed for housing in the 1860s, food, old clothes and second-hand goods have been sold here on open stalls; indeed many of the same families are still involved. Recent com-mercial development of the antique trade might easily have changed the character of the upper market, but it will be a long time before the old ways die among the fruit stalls, and their traditionalism extends a protective hand to the neighbouring antique stalls.

There is, of course, nothing peaceful or quiet about this part of the market, with the stallholders shouting out the prices of their tomatoes or apples and calling for more supplies. On Saturdays there is a constant stream of shoppers from dawn until dusk, and all along the left-hand side of the road piles of crates and baskets are assembled by the assistants, cabbages trimmed and potatoes sieved to replenish the stock on the stalls.

It is encouraging to see that many of the fruit stalls are run by young men who have not yet been tempted away from the flourishing little businesses of their fathers and grandfathers. Indeed the communal spirit is immensely strong among these families and the sorrows or joys of one are shared by all. Recently the senior member of one family died and her coffin was carried by six stallholders through the whole length of the market; her old stall was covered in a glorious display of wreaths from all the local shops, and the usually bustling market was transfixed in respectful silence as the coffin passed.

The shops also have a varied character. The butchers do an amazingly brisk trade, with one selecting the meat, another cutting it up, a third weighing and wrapping, and a fourth finding pickings for dog-owners and advising inexperienced young wives how to cook their Sunday joints.

The Portobello Road is full of accidental contrasts. A vast and impersonal Tesco supermarket extends a neon portal over the roof of a battered old fruit stall, both serving the same cosmopolitan populace. The revived Electric Cinema offers an esoteric selection of Japanese features, American underground films and some modern classics to its grateful members, while up the road 'Leisure Time' entices a different clientele in to play bingo at 5p a card. But at their lower ends even these contrasting intel-lectual and working-class cultures overlap, as a down-and-out, drunken labourer begs his entry to the warmth of the Electric, and a semi-stoned film-fanatic floats into the bingo hall, mesmerized by the air-blown fountain of coloured balls.

Travelling northwards down the Portobello one is led further and further into committed hippiedom. The first sign of the alternative culture, apart from beards and beads, is the 'Dog Shop' which introduces its phallic snout and multi-coloured façade in among the fruit stalls. After inspection of their assorted jeans and joss-sticks, the next stop is at one of the hippie meccas of London, the Ceres Bakery and Natural Food Shop. This supplies all the basic ingredients for 'organic living', which include 'raisins and green figs from Afghanistan', 'wild, sweet apricots' described as 'the basic food of the Hunzas of Kashmir', and all sorts of fruit and vegetables grown in this country without the use of toxic sprays. The credentials of the macrobiotic food cult are displayed on a poster: 'Macro means great; the Maka of Sanscrit. Biotic means life or way of life. Macrobiotic means a great and wonderful life.' If the Tassajara Bread Book does not convince you of the healthful effects of kneading dough, then follow up the open invitation on a notice-board by the door to join Guru Nanak in a pancake breakfast.

Of the North Kensington area's large and attractive coloured population, many families have lived in the neighbourhood for two or even three generations, and their Saturday scene centres round the Jamaican Pattie Company, three doors away from the Ceres Bakery and serving the best patties in London. From a stall outside, Reggae music plays to the crowd of would-be Rastafarians as they eagerly thumb through the stacks of records. Up above are posters of Jimmie Cliff and Janet Bartley, the stars of *The Harder They Come*, which has already enjoyed three riotous returns to the Notting Hill Gaumont Cinema.

From Tavistock Road to Golborne Road trading in food-stuffs is prohibited and the streets are immediately lined with traders in second-hand clothes, electrical goods and other odds and ends. A tribe of Indian street-sellers brighten the scene with their fabrics and handicrafts. But for antique-hunters the attraction of this area is the market beneath the Westway flyover, run by the North Kensington Amenity Trust. The majority of goods on this jumble of stalls tend to be Victorian or later, but keen eyes have spotted period fire-irons, fenders and other items which stallholders can easily misjudge, not thinking of them as 'antiques'. The stalls here have a definite charm and quality of their own, indeed the best stall on the Portobello for porcelain door-knobs and other door furniture competes for attention with the Gypsy stall selling copies of Jeremy Sandford's newspaper *Romany Drom*.

Every Friday and Saturday pop-groups or theatre companies give free entertainment in the Westway Theatre alongside Portobello Green. The

'Ooh, interesting, 1658 Birmingham – or is that a Bristol mark?'

The Portobello Road extends for over a mile into the hippier community of North Kensington, and pop bands perform every Saturday in a makeshift arena below the motorway flyover at the junction of Cambridge Gardens

The extensive fruit and vegetable market at the bottom end of the Portobello operates every day except Sundays. All the produce is marvellously fresh, and half the price of West End fruiterers

Tube rail runs low beside the stage and the weighty amplification of the music competes with the irregular percussion of the passing trains. On sunny afternoons a colourful hippie crowd gathers on the grass to watch the show, or queues at the door of Prince Gypsy Petulengro Lee's mobile palmist's van. Further down the road old age pensioners file out of the Council's 'Luncheon Club for Senior Citizens'.

In this relaxed environment even the implausible hand-outs seem momentarily feasible, like the invitation to consult Madame Cynthia of Willesden whose 'Palm, Card, Crystal Ball and Phrenologist Readings' are claimed to solve all problems. One may even be tempted to give alms to the Church of Aphrodite Pandemos (Convenor, the Reverend F. F. Pawlowski, DD) and so help supply the acid and psychedelics for at least one of the five million to trip in pop festivals later on in the summer.

Leaving behind the stalls of Hare Krishna and the Wayfinders' Youth Club, one comes to some interesting junk and bric-a-brac stalls, including a good second-hand bookseller. Then, just past the Convent of the Little Sisters of the Poor, comes a marvellous mini-section of the market. First a shop called Sunset Boulevard presents a shimmering collection of dresses from the twenties and thirties, potential for a stunning wardrobe. Near by, a stall offers a companion assortment of extravagant costume-jewellery all of which is cheap, most modern and some wearable. And next door at No. 308, P. H. Forest's antique shop is worth a careful browse as good items of Victoriana like Minton jardinières sometimes appear at half the price of the grander shops.

On a different but no less significant track, Exchange and Mart Fair across the road has the best bargains in second-hand bicycles for all North London. Finally, if anyone is looking for somewhere to watch the Saturday football on television he certainly should know of a septuagenarian wizard who conjures perfect pictures on both BBC and ITV from battered television sets on his stall outside Forest's shop; the sets are all less than £10 each, and the owner would do better by passing a hat round the crowd of onlookers.

The official area of street trading on the Portobello terminates at the crossing of Golborne Road, which has its own street market ending at the railway bridge. People say that this small stretch of market is like the Portobello used to be before the war, when dealers in all sorts of second-hand junk as well as cheap modern products rubbed shoulders with the fruiterers. The Golborne Market is similar to the Church Street Market off the Edgware Road but far smaller, its principal function being to serve the rather poor community living in the area. A few canny dealers are found even so far down, notably two young silver sharks who search far and wide for discoveries that will impress their parents on the established

Portobello stalls. Preparing to turn back towards Notting Hill one is suddenly confronted with a surrealistic scene. Under the auspices of the remarkable Reverend Peake, the Golborne Road Church is transformed every Saturday into a crowded bingo hall, the altar being hidden beneath dolls, crates of beer, and all the other secular prizes. But then, the constant possibility of surprises is the principal delight of a Saturday visit to the Portobello Market.

The stallholders and dealers

At the last survey the total number of antique stallholders and shop-owners on the Portobello exceeded two thousand, and since then several new arcades have opened and others have been redesigned to accommodate more stalls. This has produced an endless diversity; if almost anything can be bought somewhere on the Portobello on a Saturday morning, almost anyone could be manning a stall.

Though the Portobello has responded quickly and easily to the surge of popular interest in collecting antiques, a healthy proportion of the market remains in the hands of the original market families. Both Alice Carter, who runs Alice's, the general shop by Denbigh Close, and her husband were born on the Portobello. Alice's father is Shoggy Warren, who used to run a coal-cum-junk shop on the corner of Bolton Road and Portobello. He still spends one day a week in the shop, and no doubt also advises his son on the running of his recently opened Portobello Road premises. In a way it is hardly surprising that Alice's Victorian furniture and furnishings are distinctive and original, for the family were handling this kind of merchandise for years before it was taken up by fashionable designers. Indeed, they were among the first to make a speciality of brass bedsteads and stripped furniture, both of which emerge free of paint and rust from brother Pete's caustic soda bath.

Across the road, Roger's Antique Arcade is owned and run by a second-generation Portobello trader, and both the W. Jones and Hildreth complexes are successful local ventures. All these families are justifiably proud of the 'Lane', and their sturdy, experienced outlook does much to protect the market from the slick commercialism of newer rivals. The old families are even a little critical that their butcher, G. Portwine, has converted his shop into an arcade, though he has left the splendid façade intact.

Susan Garth, the owner of the 'Red Lion', has been promising the newspapers a twenty-first birthday party for the arcade since 1972, but many would deny her extravagant claim to be the 'mother of the Portobello Road' and to have 'started the ball rolling'. Certainly all the big arcade owners, especially those as vociferous as Miss Garth, have contributed to the progress of the Portobello; but far more important are old-timers like 'Lil', whose new stall in the Red Lion is still on the same spot she claimed in 1951. When Lil began selling jewellery in the Red Lion hers was the only antique stall, indeed her only neighbours were the 'totters' of silk stockings and similar goods. The stalls were unlighted, and a dark waste-land extended behind her into the disused warehouse; sometimes not a single buyer visited her stall for weeks on end. Now of course things are different, and life is both busier and easier. But Lil regrets the passing of those early years, complaining bitterly of the popularization of antiques, the television programmes and masses of books that have turned collecting from a private hobby into a fashionable pursuit.

Lil is not alone in seeking to keep competitiveness at bay in the Portobello, for she has stallholder-allies like gypsy Dan who cling to the old style of market dealing. In all weathers Dan bares his tattooed arms to the elbow and takes up his commanding position near the Westbourne Park Road crossroads. All manner of oddments are piled in deliberate disarray to encourage other dealers into thinking they will unearth a bargain. Resting his vast bulk on a complaining stool Dan communicates his innate good humour to all his immediate surroundings, and measuring his charm against the size of his belly, it is still just possible to believe the popular gossip about his amorous escapades throughout the Southern counties.

Outside Hildreth's office sits an Irish dealer in silver, watches and gold, whose seething indignation against 'them yellow-bellies and layabouts' (Indians and hippies) contrasts with Dan's cheerful acceptance of the influx of clothes and craft dealers into the Portobello. But then, the Irishman's style of dealing is completely different from Dan's, for all his business is done with other traders on the market, and the crowds of souvenir-hunting tourists are just in the way as far as he is concerned. Many regulars commission him to find particular gold fitments for jewellery, and he has a busy trade in gold watch-chains, called 'Alberts', which he weighs and counter-weighs in his arthritic, nicotine-stained fingers before offering a price. Inside Hildreth's Arcade another old stallholder trades with a very different style. Maudie Cutter made her childhood début on the London stage before the first world war, and for many years now has used her theatrical experience to create a marvellous aura around her stall of feather boas, ostrich-feather fans and outrageous hats. Maudie gleefully persuades her customers to try on all sorts of extravagant costumes as she spins yarns about her times on the boards. Though her dramatic hats are not at all expensive, Maudie's performances at the stall seldom secure the sales they deserve.

These established regulars naturally have an appeal all of their own, but many of the newer stallholders have a similar feeling for the traditional

Dan bares his tattooed arms at a central stall on the Portobello

qualities which distinguish the Portobello. One of my favourite dealers still keeps a list of the twelve articles given to him by his grandmother with which he started trading on the Portobello. Each week he earned enough to pay the rent of the stall and to buy more stock, and after five years part-time trading he had saved over £2,000 with a capital outlay of nothing at all. Since then he has turned to the trade full time, but he still operates just from stalls in the Westbourne Antique Arcade on Saturdays and the New Caledonian on Fridays.

Some irate professionals on the Road claim that more then 70 per cent of the stallholders are just part-timers, but, if this is true, it certainly has no evil effects, for many of the non-professionals bring an unconventionality of taste that adds new dimensions to the trading scene. Many resting or retired actors and writers end up with Portobello stalls, and their search for enjoyment as much as profit creates its own amusement. One stallholder in the Red Lion is seldom seen without the pair of spectacles he wore in a brief appearance in the last scene of the film *Clockwork Orange*; and Jeff Borsack proudly decorates his jewellery stall with press cuttings and photographs of his comedy appearances with Frankie Howerd and other stars.

But theatrical appearances are not confined to the actor-stallholders, as the inimitable Jean Carrau takes a hammer to his paintings on metal and proves their indestructibility. Carrau's story-line depends entirely on the direction of the wind at his stall outside the bottom end of the Portobello Antique Arcade; one day in reply to questions about the artist, Carrau will say 'he is alive and well at seventy-three in San Francisco', while in summer he admits to having painted them himself on inspiration from Miró, Chagall and other modern artists. In the eighteen or so years that Carrau has been on the Portobello he has sold over two thousand paintings to clients from all over the world.

Olaf O'Blayney Barnet, like Jean Carrau, also sells his own work on the Portobello, but in the rather more comfortable surroundings of his upstairs 'Collectors Gallery', virtually next door to the Portobello Arms. The proximity of the pub is not purely incidental, for during Saturday trading large quantities of wine and beer are consumed by the painter and the young artists whom he befriends. Only a small number of the paintings on view are by Barnet himself, but little attempt is made to sell any of them. 'There's more upstairs but it's all rubbish' is one of his favourite comments. Aggravated by people he considers either uninteresting or uninterested, Barnet will bang a vast dinner-gong until the startled tourists retreat down the

Years of bending over market stalls has taken its toll on this charming old couple inspecting a filigree silver tea set in the cheerful chaos of Dan's pitch

stairs. But with struggling artists, or with collectors with a genuine feeling for painting, Barnet makes every effort to help.

Some stallholders who market anything and everything that comes into fashion, regardless of age or quality, have a roguish appeal. Many of these itinerant street traders switch from Goss china to Indian textiles and back again with every swing of fashion. At a stall outside Collectors Corner there is little effort made to disguise the modernity of the Tiffany brass belt buckles; they are attractive at the price and large consignments leave for the States. American customs applied a metallurgical test to a recent crate-load and amazed both the buyer and seller by ruling that 40 per cent were old!

Collectors Corner itself is one of the oldest covered markets on the Portobello, and its dealers have a fine reputation. Stallholders like Betty Brandt and Alexander Raghinsky add an impression of aristocratic expertise to the good-humoured amateurism of much of the Road. But an observant newcomer to the Portobello will soon discover that Raghinsky's stall of 18th-century pottery and porcelain, with its hand-written descriptive labels, is not the only place where quality is appreciated. One only has to glance at Lucie Campbell and her stall in Harris's Arcade to realize that there are still stallholders on the Portobello concerned with more than just the passing tourist-trade in pointless knick-knacks. Dotted in and about the arcades are many such people, whose expertise rivals that of the best West End dealers; indeed, so do their prices in many cases.

For sheer style and quality of dealing no one on the Portobello can rival Geoffrey Van, for although the motley Portobello crowd is encouraged to move with customary freedom throughout his shop, there is still almost a museum atmosphere created by the sumptuousness and rarity of the long 16th-century walnut tables, the polychrome Gothic figures and Hispano-moresque lustre plates. Although Geoffrey Van and his son are the only Portobello dealers in things of such an early date, other dealers have established themselves as equally prominent experts in other fields. There is for example Judy Fox, fifty yards up the hill from the Vans' shop, who concentrates entirely on English pottery from the period 1870 to 1920, or Mrs Collins with her prominent Art Nouveau stall in Shepherd's Antique Arcade. Indeed the women dealers tend to be pioneers on the Portobello, for Mrs Collins was one of the original market enthusiasts for Art Nouveau, and now Judy Fox leads the way in English ceramics of this same period.

There are many more devoted experts amongst the stallholders who could be mentioned: people like 'Mr Satsuma', in the Westbourne Antique Arcade, who valued this Japanese pottery long before its recent fashionable revival, or Alexandra, in the Corner Portobello Antique Supermarket, who is irrepressibly enthusiastic about her stylish but inexpensive Art

Parrot and polyphon travel with Wally from Land's End to John o' Groats, but seldom miss a Saturday on the Portobello where they engage in friendly rivalry with all the other street performers and buskers

Nouveau collections. Though the Portobello Market is more than just a concourse of dedicated collectors and dealers, the continued existence of these enthusiastic experts provides a solid backbone without which the 'antique' scene would quickly disintegrate into an undistinguished second-hand bazaar.

The street performers

The Portobello Market and its Saturday crowds attract a host of street performers. Some favourites, like Wally with his parrot and polyphon, and Alisha, a charming ballad-singer, have been coming regularly to the

Buyers at market stalls need have no fear that they are also paying for the cost of the premises, or merely being seduced by sophisticated presentation

Portobello for many years, and these regulars are supported by an ever-changing band of musicians, so there is always something going on. The only danger to this impromptu street entertainment is the constant efforts of the local policemen to disperse the performers who lack licences, which is practically all of them; but the buskers keep returning to add an attractive extra dimension to the Portobello scene.

On a fine spring day almost every street corner is occupied by a folk-singer, whose admiring girl-friend proffers a collecting bag to the passing crowds. No doubt many of these musicians are the same that haunt subways and Tube stations during the week; at their week-day pitches they so often appear sad and ineffectual, but in the lively atmosphere of the Portobello they seem more like wandering troubadours.

Some performances are memorable by any standards. There is a young American violinist whose womenfolk set out a collection of handmade clothes on the pavement while he erects his music stand, and hangs a

The juxtaposition of this weird ventriloquist's dummy, a bust of Abraham Lincoln and a blaring phonograph is enough to frighten any child

Piles of cardboard boxes and newspaper at the end of the day show just how healthy trade is on the markets. Soon the dust carts will come rumbling down the Portobello Road to restore the mile of street market to temporary order

notice on the railings, 'Music is a beautiful way to start the day.' In the early morning business bustle he launches into the whole of a Mozart violin concerto, and neither the surrounding clamour nor the almost total lack of attention of the antique-hunters can disturb his concentrated performance. Of the folk-singers and guitarists the best is a girl with long brown hair called Alisha, who normally plays at the mouth of Vernon's Yard, not far from the monkey photographers. On first seeing her, singing ballads shyly to the ground, one imagines that this is her first street performance, but in fact she is an experienced entertainer, and has long delighted Portobello regulars with her complex classical fingering of the guitar. Alisha quite often joins up with other musicians, and her duets with a flautist called Jeff gather crowds that block the road completely.

Street musicians like Alisha can be classed almost as professionals in the regularity of their appearances, whereas many of the others are just itinerant American hippies, begging their way round the world. Quarrels frequently arise between these interlopers and the old street buskers as they clash over prize pitches. The 'Earl of Mustard', a tap dancer, almost came to blows with one guitarist who demanded that they 'have respect for one another ... we are both in the same game'; at this Mustard exploded with rage and accused the young hippie of never having done an honest day's work in his life, whereas he was doing a twelve hour day with his feet. The Earl of Mustard's principal territory is in the West End where he dances for the cinema queues and departing theatre audiences. He is happiest when accompanied by a one-man-band artist, Scott, self-styled 'King of the Buskers'; dressed in a crimson military tunic and balaclava helmet, Mustard stampedes through a five-minute tap-routine that includes a repertoire of grotesque face-pulls, rude noises and haphazard blasts on a brass hooter. His mood is less abandoned when, dressed in black tails and accompanied by a hand-cranked gramophone placed on the pavement beside him, he ruefully harangues his audience as it disappears into the crowd when the performance has ended and the hat is passed round.

There is often a choice of one-man bands during a Portobello Saturday, Scott and his friend Mac being the most regular. Their contortionist cacophony of guitar, drum, cymbals, whistles and mouth-organ starts ambitiously but tends to deteriorate into the tune 'Freight Train'; the presence of a watchful policeman calls to mind the cartoon of a serious young 'Bobby' leading off a one-man-band artist with instruments tied to every part of his body, the caption threatening, 'If you don't come *quietly* ...!' Scott and Mac are both tremendous street entertainers, but the best 'bandsman' in musical terms is another professional called Mike Griggs, who adds a tambourine to the normal ensemble, and includes a remarkably wide variety of songs.

The road is especially full of musical sounds at the height of the summer. Serious young men in tennis shorts and girls in cotton dresses struggle with a temperamental Edwardian barrel-organ at the corner of West-bourne Grove and the Portobello; their enthusiasm is irresistible, and the Christian Aid collecting boxes quickly fill. The strangest, and in many ways the most alluring, sound on the Portobello is the lilting tune of the Langley ocarina, a closed clay pipe which derives from an Aztec instrument and has a country-innocent, Pan-like sound. But the best-known music of the whole market comes from Wally's polyphon. Wally is the sailor-like figure with a parrot on his arm who wanders up and down the road turning the tin discs on a gaily-painted polyphon hanging round his neck; as the parrot is considerably more talkative than its owner, it is difficult to dis-cover the secrets of a strange life written in the fixed creases of Wally's face. Perhaps the truth would turn out to be far more mundane than the stories suggested by parrot and dress.

All these buskers and beggars are merely Saturday visitors, but Notting Hill does possess its own resident street player, the thin, small old man who often sits in the Tube station wearing a black bowler hat on which is chalked 'Spider, 21 Today'. He usually just sits there in the warm, talking to himself or playing the mouth-organ, and anyone who drops a coin in his lap is instantly greeted with a firm shake of the hand and a garbled thank-you. In other moods Spider can be rather frightening as he prances about the Portobello in his black tailcoat, wielding a white cane and swearing violently at innocent tourists. At his best, however, Spider is the most aristocratic of buskers, eccentric but not mad, funny but not pathetic; and his greatest charm is in his love for the children of the 'Lane'. One cold, windy evening last winter, as all the stalls were packing up, Spider came dancing up the road playing his mouth-organ, followed by three tiny children attached to his tailcoat. Every now and then the bizarre group came to a halt and Spider gave the three little boys further instruc-tion in the hopping steps with which they were progressing up the hill. They finally stopped near the top and Spider took his friends aside, fished into his pocket, patted each of them on the head, stuffed a five-penny bit in their grubby hands and said 'And now piss off the lot of you.'

There is always the chance of the unexpected happening on Saturdays in the Portobello, and however many years one may have been 'doing' the market this feeling of excitement remains. The surprise of the day may come simply in discovering an unusual addition to one's collection or from bumping into a particularly amusing character in the ever-changing crowd. And if all else fails there will always be the street entertainers like the Earl of Mustard or Alisha the ballad-singer who ask for and receive a direct human response that makes the disappointments of the day fall away.

The beauty of this experience is brought out most clearly in the occasional visits of two marvellous old fair-ground performers. Stripped to the waist, these two sixty-year-olds go through an extraordinarily inept escapologist's routine with such enthusiasm and panache that by the end of the performances even the jeering local kids are seen sheepishly throwing coins into the centre of the makeshift street stage. So long as the vigour of street life in the Portobello can be maintained in this way the market itself will continue to be a place of real distinction.

The future of the Portobello

Sadly, the traditional character of the Portobello is threatened on all sides. The recent commercialization of the whole antique scene has been mentioned several times earlier. Of more immediate concern are the Borough Council's disturbing proposals for the redevelopment of the Colville-Tavistock area of so-called 'Rotting Hill'.

In May 1973 Kensington and Chelsea Council published a proposal for the demolition of the entire block containing the Duke of Wellington pub and the Electric Cinema, and its replacement with a modern shopping precinct, car park and office space. While the adjacent fruit market would still continue to function, the traditional qualities and character of the market would disappear for ever in developments of this sort.

On the whole the community seems relatively well equipped to protect its favourite institutions as well as the interests of the individual. There is widespread opposition to the destruction of the Electric, which was in 1905 the second custom-built cinema in London. Both structure and decoration are in their original condition, and the Electric Cinema Club has been revitalized to show esoteric modern films to its active membership.

Indeed North Kensington locals have a long history of militancy, beginning with their opposition to the Hippodrome Race Course built in 1836 with its southern entrance on what is now the Pembridge and Kensington Park Road crossing. As the boundaries contravened a public footpath large sections of the public demanded free entry to the June Meeting of 1837 and through their large numbers successfully 'defiled the atmosphere' for the rich racing fraternity.

More recently, at a public meeting three councillors were held hostage overnight because they refused to give any direct answers to the residents' questions concerning the fate of Council tenants.

Although the antique market in the Portobello Road has grown far beyond the limits of the community, its lively character is still both conditioned and protected by the individuality and concern of the people of North Kensington.

A thinly disguised West End dealer closely examines a silver spoon to make sure that the mark is completely genuine

2 Bermondsey: The New Caledonian Market

Friday at Bermondsey

Before the last war the old Caledonian Market enjoyed the privilege of a special site up on Copenhagen Fields, Islington, and regulars who remember this seething square mile of activity find it difficult to adjust to the New Caledonian Market down in Bermondsey. Many traditional market families were unable to revive their businesses in new surroundings after the losses and disruption of the war, and even more significant, the whole antique trade has developed so rapidly in recent years that dealing from market stalls has become a totally different occupation. Victorian bric-a-brac even on street stalls is now big business, and supporters of the traditional markets feel that the New Caledonian has become just another scene in the bourgeois pantomime of fashionable collecting.

But although styles have changed, the Bermondsey Market, middle class and commercial as it undoubtedly is, still possesses a mystique and an impetus that links it with its rich past. The unforced individuality of the stallholders, the vigour of the early morning scene, the quality of much of the trading – all these can still excite even the most sceptical of visitors.

Nor have all the traditions of Copenhagen Fields been left behind in Islington. Trading begins even earlier than in the old days, and only the lure of a bargain and the shrill call of an alarm-clock draws us North Londoners from our warm beds on the long trek across town. A Bermondsey regular may attempt to sleep late, but his dreams will be cruelly punctuated by visions of rival collectors gloating over countless discoveries on his own favourite stalls; for there are as many bargains on the New Caledonian as there were on the old. Whatever the weather, it is an early start on Friday mornings.

True, success can never be guaranteed amid the cut-throat competition, and many of the best goods will have changed hands a couple of times and then disappeared into deep hold-alls before 6 o'clock in the morning. But despite the hardship of an early rise and the sternness of professional competition, a visit to Bermondsey is always worth the effort, for the simple reason that the New Caledonian every Friday morning is the meeting-place of all the middle-men in the south of England antique trade; to be a regular visitor is the collector's opportunity of tapping the supply of antiques at its prime source.

On spring mornings it is already half light as we scurry south of the river, surrounded by a loud chorus of sparrows and starlings not yet overwhelmed by the daytime roar of traffic. In the unaccustomed quiet of the early morning the few sounds are magnified to eerie proportions as cars and lorries career wildly through the empty, echoing streets. It is with a sense of relief that one leaves the unfamiliarly clear street air for the protective rumble of the Underground, a reassurance that the power of the city continues unabated; and it is a pleasure to bask in the luxury of deserted stations, reading the morning paper still hot from the Fleet Street presses.

The mingling of a few bearded professionals with the first-shift workers suggests that the train is approaching its market destination; this is confirmed by an excited Italian couple decoding the complexities of the Northern Line with the aid of a pocket guide. Nothing deters the real enthusiast.

The view on emerging from Borough Station is by no means encouraging, and a ten-minute walk down Long Lane reveals dilapidated warehouses and terraced streets which are hardly improved upon by modern high-rise flats; yet excitement mounts until one rounds the last corner and comes suddenly on the buzzing market hive. On a cold morning the two large blocks of open stalls are shrouded in a fog of warm human breath; and a shout of excitement has to be suppressed as one dives indiscriminately into one of the many narrow passages between the stalls.

It is difficult to describe what the visitor can expect to see, since the form and mood of the market depend on the season and the weather. In winter the market looks at first sight like the deck of a mid-Victorian sailing-ship carrying emigrants to Australia, with the canvases flapping in the wind and hurricane lamps shedding a tremulous glow over the muffled stallholders. Winter or summer, one factor remains constant, namely the quiet professionalism of the unhurried but purposeful activity among the stalls. For despite the casualness of appearances, an experienced glint in the eye and a confident handling of goods instantly reveals the predominance of practised dealers. By 6 o'clock at least half the stalls are laden with objects of all description, and latecomers hastily transfer the paraphernalia of the market from the temporary disarray of the parked cars. Immediately an expectant group gathers about stalls with a reputation for producing novelties each week. Just as in the early hours on the Portobello, privileged customers are offered an appropriate box to unpack on their own, and hundreds of pounds can change hands before private buyers have so much as glanced at a porcelain plate. After this first rushed exchange, the goods for sale can be viewed at greater leisure, and there is time to enjoy the whole varied scene.

For no particular reason the strongest part of Bermondsey Market has built up in the centre of the Abbey Street block, bounded at the northern end by the tall wooden hoarding which encloses the barrow store. This part of the market is habitually the most crowded, and on rainy days the canvas roofs on the tightly packed stalls block out the sky almost completely. Perhaps it is just a romantic imagination looking for sinister undercurrents, but the 'heavies' seem to gather there in close huddles, their expressionless faces giving no clue to the nature of their conversations muttered through half-clenched tobacco-stained teeth. The spectators turn away to smile to themselves when one of the 'heavies' precipitates a cascade of water down his neck from an accidentally dislodged flat-roof reservoir. On a summer's morning the rising sun's rays light the open stalls completely, and this vision of a shady underworld dissolves into the improbable fantasy it really is.

All along the Bermondsey Square side of this block battered vans have disgorged stacks of Victorian furniture and brassware. Business is actually over for most of these furniture dealers, for despite the protests of sleepless residents, the bulk of their trading has been completed between midnight and three in the morning, and many van-loads will already have caught the early Channel ferry for quick sales in Italy or the expanding German market. Many of the lorries are in fact collecting, not unloading at all; but some of the export traders from Westbourne Grove can still be seen rushing about the market, marking their last purchases down in outsize order-books. There may even be some serviceable sets of dining chairs left over at a reasonable price for the private buyer.

Halfway down the same side of the market one of the most likable characters on the New Caledonian plies his trade. Jack to some, William to others, but Bill to most, dispenses piping hot coffee and not-so-hot-dogs from a steaming van parked by the market entrance, and for more than twelve hours, starting at 4.30 in the morning, he keeps up a seemingly endless chatter to complement the equally inexhaustible supply of tea and coffee. Some regulars queue up, not merely for coffee, but also for the pleasure of exchanging extravagant insults with the irrepressible Bill, with his rubicund face, perpetual gap-toothed smile and shock of sandy-coloured hair. The fears and foibles of all his regulars are known to Bill, who invents thoughtful ways of first cheering them up and then keeping them amused.

Standing there by the hot-dog van, trying to hold the scalding tea in a plastic cup, one sees market life in all its varied forms pass by. A snappily dressed silver dealer dangling a teapot or cream-jug from each finger threads his way through the parked cars to his own vehicle, a gleaming Rolls-Royce. The Laurel and Hardy pair of Market Inspectors stride efficiently about finding spare stalls for newcomers, and exercising their considerable powers with a far from comical panache. There may already be a few determined tourists about and these are easily distinguished by their slightly perplexed expressions and by their louder, more assertive voices.

On the southern block of the New Caledonian Market traders set out their goods early on a fine morning. Despite the apparent calm, dealing is fast and furious from soon after 5 o'clock every Friday

Meanwhile the dealers drift from stall to stall, some quickly filling baskets with their specialities and others just stopping occasionally to bargain over a random rarity. All the time regulars dart about for a chat with friends, the Friday market being a time for sharing news as well as exchanging goods.

At about 7 o'clock, the official opening time of the market, David Styles puts on his street show at a stall facing the Bermondsey Street block of the market. The 'props' vary from the normal haul of silver and jewellery to an outrageous pile of junk, but he always gathers an excited crowd as new goods are guaranteed each week. Helped by a couple of tight-lipped henchmen who keep their eyes skinned for pilferers, Styles empties his bags and boxes on to the worn velvet cloth in indiscriminate heaps, into which immediately delve countless grasping hands. Nothing is priced beforehand, and customers merely hand over their choice, while Styles calls out and adds up the prices item by item. The customer then leaves out the unwanted pieces, haggles over the remainder, and eventually a wad of notes disappears into the top pocket of Styles' combat jacket. Styles' performance never falters. 'How much is this ring?' 'Six quid.' 'But it was a fiver two minutes ago.' 'Then you should've bought it,' is the unanswerable reply. Everything is a great game. A customer explodes at the price of a silver-plated teapot with lead repaired base and new spout, only to be silenced with, 'Well, look at the price of lead these days.'

Across the road in the second market block the stalls are less tightly packed together but equally full of possibilities. Practically every Friday an old man wanders this way towards his car bearing some piece of Georgian furniture which he has miraculously extracted from the plethora of Victoriana. At the far end on Bermondsey Street itself an old London taxi and a stall display a bewildering assortment of battered oddments. Periodically Sid, the proprietor, disappears into the passenger seat and hurls out a further selection of clothes, comics and coal scuttles. On fine mornings his rheumatism clears sufficiently for him to enjoy the task of polishing his taxi's bonnet with suitable respect, and later, giving up the unequal struggle to persuade anyone actually to purchase his headless plaster figure of Aphrodite, he lies back sleepily among the flotsam and jetsam of the back seat.

Years ago the old Caledonian had a reputation for the painless disposal of stolen goods, and there are still always some police in the vicinity in case of emergency. Recently a young couple successfully identified a piece of their stolen silver on a stall, and a policeman was obliged to invite the stallholder to accompany him down to the station. Pale and embarrassed, the young couple were followed by the critical stares of the protective crowd, and even the policeman nervously sucked his helmet strap as they ran the gauntlet of the stalls. Nowadays the police raids concentrate on

The benevolent Market Inspectors have obviously been presented with a difficult problem by this lady, but it would be rare to find this busy pair completely at a loss for an answer

the illegally parked cars which soon get towed away, to the great inconvenience of the careless stallholder.

While the principal activity of the day is in the open street market, visitors should not ignore the stalls housed in 251–5 Long Lane, which the proprietor has cheekily called the 'Bermondsey Antique Market' as the name had not previously been officially registered. On a cold day the warmth inside and the hot sausage rolls quickly revive drooping spirits, though sometimes the more potent medicine of the Hand and the Marigold may be needed when the pub doors are obligingly opened at 7.30 a.m. In no way could space be more fully employed in this indoor Bermondsey Market, where it may take many visits for collectors to locate the last few stalls concealed at the end of cat-walks beneath the rafters. Up in the eaves some reasonable prints jostle for space with battered fruit machines, and in another back room a stallholder snores peacefully in the only comfortable, or indeed saleable, chair in sight. The beams up there are coated with thick black tar which has formed miniature stalactites, giving the jumbled rooms the appearance of underground grottoes.

Two young enthusiasts have already caught the collecting bug, as they eagerly sort through some coins and medals on their way to school

Perhaps a still from a Fellini film?

One of the delights of the markets is the ease of communication between totally divergent characters, shown by the friendship of these three regulars

At half past nine with the sun just beginning to warm up the morning air, the day's work is already over for one Bermondsey stallholder's assistant

By 9.30 the weight of business is over, and stallholders cease trying to combine the conflicting demands of selling their own goods with the desire to search others' stalls for their own speciality; instead they settle down comfortably at their own stall to chat to the neighbours and to deal haphazardly with the private buyers and tourists who gradually begin to outnumber the professionals. The visiting dealers smartly engage the tourists' taxis to return them and their new-found treasures to the West End. Indeed a number of stallholders themselves tend to pack up between 9 and 10, but there is always a queue of new traders for these vacated stalls.

Last call for many dealers is the Rose Dining Rooms, just round the corner of Long Lane and Bermondsey Street, for large helpings of bacon, egg and mushrooms. There can be no greater pleasure for the collector than tucking into a hearty breakfast secure in the knowledge that the 'discovery of the day', which has by now been whispered twice through the market and thrice round the Rose Dining Rooms, is safely cradled in his own pocket.

'It was working yesterday, sir.' Stallholders seldom offer a direct guarantee, and, anyway, a sensible collector should trust only his own judgement

Caledonian traditions

The original Caledonian Market was founded in 1855 when a large area on Copenhagen Fields, Islington, was walled in and developed principally for the sale of cattle. But the tradition of street markets has a far longer history in Islington, which was the first stop from London on the trek up the Great North Road, and therefore became a natural rallying and victualling point for pedlars and travellers alike.

It was for the cattle merchants that a special market was built by James Bunning, and officially opened in 1855 by Albert, Prince Consort, who might not have approved had he known that no less than four public houses were licensed inside the market for the cattle drovers alone. The cattle merchants were unable to keep the market to themselves for long and, by the end of the century, tradition had established that Friday in the Caledonian was reserved for all the cheap commercial traders and junk men of London, many of whom lived in Islington itself. In *A Wanderer in London* of 1906, E. V. Lucas described a Friday morning visit to the Caledonian on a bitterly cold day when the signs of greatest activity were to be seen around the open braziers and hot-chestnut men dotted about the vast open space. On such a day Lucas found it impossible to understand why antique dealers proclaimed the merits of a market in which the sellers of second-hand corsets considerably outnumbered even the junk dealers, 'and if there is a less engaging sight then a huddle of corsets I hope never to see it'. Although Lucas had been advised to arrive early, when stallholders hastened to off-load silver and jewellery of some quality and doubtful ownership, he nevertheless claimed to have seen 'not only nothing that a collector of any taste would buy, but nothing that any but a confirmed and undiscriminating kleptomaniac would steal'. Similar thoughts may even occur today on a particularly damp and depressing morning on the New Caledonian.

The 'antique' heyday of the Caledonian was in the twenties and thirties. From 1924 the market was closed to the cattle on Tuesdays as well; meanwhile Friday morning at the market had become a feature in the calendar of fashionable London, with processions of gleaming new motor-cars bringing social mannequins to parade across the cobble-stones.

As the Caledonian was entirely enclosed by railings a toll system of entry could be enforced, and poor traders, carrying as large a load as they could manage, just paid for their entry and hawked their goods around the square mile of market, or settled down hopefully on the cobbles. A larger fee was charged to wheel in a proper stall, and those wanting a plum pitch had to send a 'runner' through the crush at the opening of the gates to reserve the chosen spot. Half the battle was won on engaging a good 'runner', and the term is still used in the trade today to describe the men who travel about the country buying particular items on commission for wealthy London dealers. Cheap-jacks (sellers of poor quality modern goods) and junk men predominated even in the thirties, but over the far side the 'Silver Kings' presided in considerable style amid a cacophany of mysterious whistles, calls and signs that telegraphed news such as the whereabouts of the suspicious Market Inspectors. Attendance grew to over a hundred thousand on a good day, and the Caledonian was a considerable loss when war forced its closure late in 1939.

After the war, a group of street traders put pressure on the Council to set up the New Caledonian Market by Bermondsey Square, which opened on 2 May 1949. Despite pessimism in the trade the 260 pitches were gradually filled, and the whole operation has now become such a success that there is a five-year waiting list for permanent licences. On the pre-war Caledonian Market the actual antique dealers were in a considerable minority, whereas now the new market by the site of Bermondsey Abbey has established itself as the only street market devoted exclusively to the antique trade. In this specialization the cries of the fruit-sellers and the patter of the dealers in cheap trinkets may be missed, but the quiet professionalism of trading at the New Caledonian has justifiably gained it respect and loyalty as the grass roots of the London antique trade.

The stallholders and dealers

Although a remarkable cross-section of the populace frequents the market later in the day, practically everyone there early is an antique dealer of one sort or another; even Princess Margaret on her fairly regular visits is always accompanied by a dealer friend. It is this professionalism and the closed-shop preference for dealer-trading that give Bermondsey its distinctive character. In the stallholder's eye the success of the market is assured by the inconvenience to the general public of the place and time, which preserves the New Caledonian for professional buyers.

The stallholders themselves are varied in character and background. Only a very few second- and third-generation cockney dealers are left in the market, and those still there find life progressively more difficult. In the old days the 'knockers', as they are called, used to drive their carts from door to door collecting up old bits and pieces, but now that so many more people are interested in antiques and the prices have mounted astronomically, there is little joy for an 'honest knocker'. One rosy-cheeked cockney stallholder divides the blame for her misfortunes between the part-time dealing of a local solicitor's wife and the rivalry from Oxfam; both steal her trade, one by paying over the odds from private clients, the other by encouraging donors to part freely with valuable junk. Much of the

Victorian bric-a-brac that used to be the 'knockers' daily trade now sells expensively in fashionable shops, and the old-time market people find it hard to adjust; however nothing but old age will keep them away from the market life where their families have been for generations.

In general terms, business at Bermondsey is so strong that dealers who now run two or three antique shops still find it worth keeping a stall there, and they regularly do £400–£500 trade before dawn. If other established dealers do not actually run a stall they will be regular visitors, putting in a couple of raincoat-disguised hours of intrigue before appearing in pin-striped splendour in their West End shops. But then Bermondsey stall-holders and traders come in all sizes, types and qualities, and they all contribute to the attractions of the market.

The Borough of Southwark must also be given credit for the success of the New Caledonian venture. The external market is run by a group of Market Inspectors from the Borough who spend a hectic morning dealing with everyone's problems and issuing temporary licences for the day's trading. The Borough of Southwark's market code decrees that unoccupied stalls shall be offered first to regular users of the market, so the Inspectors are protected in their favouritism towards familiar faces. On a fine day there may be twenty candidates awaiting official attention, and the new-comer can quickly be reduced to feelings of paranoia as the Inspectors

Lock's of St James's would eagerly produce a better fitting bowler hat, but a bargain is always difficult to refuse and the family album will record for ever a reckless moment.

Whether business is good or bad the stallholders are invariably in fine spirits; the
joke is only occasionally at the visitor's expense

bustle about ignoring him while hailing and being hailed in friendly
familiarity by all the regulars. (In practice the Inspectors are always fair,
and will help whenever they can; their paternal management of the stalls
also has the valuable effect of protecting the sense of intimacy and loyalty
that exists among the stallholders.)

Ian Whitfield has attempted to inject a similar feeling of shared identity
and joint interest into his 'Bermondsey Antique Market' at 251–5 Long
Lane, but his obvious and, in many ways, admirable commercial zeal
creates a different atmosphere. Whitfield has already recorded notable
successes, having graduated in three years from amateur stallholder to free-
hold owner of premises housing over 150 stalls, and he will undoubtedly be
a powerful influence on Caledonian developments. With an ex-marketing
man's propensity for generating business, Whitfield always seems to be
doing five or six things equally well at exactly the same moment, and these
may include off-loading a multi-ton consignment of jade from Peking,
insinuating his own advertising pamphlet into British Tourist Board offices,
and stockpiling every available piece of Scottish glass.

While the Inspectors and Mr Whitfield have secure control over their
areas of the market, there is nevertheless an overriding feeling of freedom
and lack of conformity throughout the New Caledonian, qualities that
have lured many people away from other jobs into the unregimented life

A worried stallholder wonders which of the watches to believe

of a street trader; for here is one of the few bread-winning occupations that lacks the intense personal rivalry of most professions. Instead of gleefully misleading an ignorant neighbour over some rare piece he asks about, a true Bermondsey man will gladly share as much information as he has, and even recommend his rival to a buyer. Friendly discussions ensue about the artistic merits of various items, or the recent development of interest in certain fields, and the whole emphasis seems to be on communal activity and the enjoyment of relaxed relationships. Indeed, to the outsider early morning Bermondsey has an atmosphere akin to a gentlemen's club, where everyone knows everyone else so well that they communicate in a verbal shorthand, and the oldest members automatically appropriate the best 'seats', receive the closest attention from the 'club servants' (the Market Inspectors), and have the best things kept aside for their first refusal; the only difference being that Bermondsey has none of the narrow-minded uniformity that petrifies such clubs.

No doubt it is the lack of ordered conformity that draws the many exotic characters, who can display their fetishes and foibles without attracting undue notice. Perhaps the most striking of these 'fetishists' is Doctor Death, or Harry the Death as he is otherwise known, who sleeps in a button-upholstered coffin and collects everything and anything to do with death. Doctor Death makes a living from dealing in jewellery, and quite regularly

Many stallholders on the markets give the impression that antique dealing is merely a stop-gap between plays, paintings or novels

Sid nonchalantly sips coffee in the sun with confidence that someone sooner or later will turn up to offer him a profit on the transfer printed cream jug, the chalet musical box or perhaps even the doll's arm which adds a macabre touch to his cluttered stall

takes a stall in the New Caledonian or on the Portobello; he normally wears tailcoat, broad homburg and leather boots, and has his long hair tied in a leather thong – all, needless to say, black. The regulars greatly enjoy his black humour. 'Oh, you'll be the death of me, Harry!' 'Promise?' – in a tone of keen anticipation.

The regular stallholders benefit from the comforting sense of belonging, and whether business is good or bad, the friendly Friday morning chatter gives a protective boost to the morale. Yet the life is by no means easy, as more and more dealers compete in purchasing diminishing stock. Admittedly, a growing number of stallholders in all the markets can only be described as part-timers and secure their principal income from other sources, but the professionals find themselves travelling further afield every week in search of new goods. Sources like the country auctions and provincial dealers have already become too expensive for regular trading. The most envied dealers are those with a constant supply of private calls, preferably in the North of England, organized through local advertising

Recently risen from a night's repose in his button-upholstered coffin, 'Harry the
Death' shares a joke with another regular at the New Caledonian

and eventually by word of mouth and a reputation for fair dealing. 'House-
clearing' is another useful source. In removing the quantities of worthless
junk the contractor may stumble across marvellous items that the auction-
eers have misguidedly turned down. One buccaneering London house-
clearer started business during hard times when, by selling all his possessions,
he raised a working capital of £65: £60 to purchase a van and £5 for
advertising. Being a non-driver he was also obliged to engage a helper
and gamble on earning at least enough to pay the wages at the end of the
week. But he need not have worried, for the second call was at a large
Kensington house where his cry of admiration for a pair of Chippendale
breakfront bookcases was mistaken by the seller for a groan of dismay at
their size, and he was promptly paid to take them away! The business
flourishes and the 'game' continues.

The best market traders develop an unfailing facility for instant price
reckoning on all objects, regardless of whether these are within their particular field of expertise; this kind of buyer may go through a whole ware-

houseful of another trader's stock in a minute or two and offer on the spot a fair price of several thousand pounds in complete confidence of making a profit on the purchase. As in all sectors of the trade the essential skill is not necessarily in recognizing the topmost value of an object, but in an ability to turn over money quickly at a profit. Thus at one end of the trade the stallholder David Styles makes an excellent living by off-loading his whole stock almost every week, finishing off the junk in an unsorted pile in Cheshire Street on a Sunday morning; while at the other end, Mallett's of Bond Street aim to turn over their whole expensive stock three times a year and therefore operate one of the most successful businesses in the West End on the same basic principle. Many times Mallett's will have eventually secured over a thousand pounds for an object that a stallholder like Styles had sold six months previously for a few hundred, and yet each in the circumstances will have secured the right price.

With so many professionals about, even an experienced private collector may be daunted, and find it difficult to overcome the feeling that there must be something wrong in the price or condition of a piece that stands unheeded by the swarm of dealers. Collectors should be emboldened by the thought that the expert-dealer in that particular field may have hurried off for breakfast at the crucial moment, leaving an unspotted bargain.

For many of the dealer-buyers the winter day begins with a long drive through dark countryside and unlit streets, terminating in battered Bermondsey, and the first hour or two of searching is carried out by the light of a pocket torch. The weekly ritual is not for the faint-hearted.

In chasing each likely stallholder to the first unpacking of the Friday offering, a dedicated dealer may tramp six or seven miles up and down the lines of stalls; and even then only an experienced eye brings satisfying buys.

Many hours later, breakfasted and warmed by the morning sun, the same dealer begins his final tour of the stalls, this time collecting the newspaper-wrapped purchases that friendly stallholders have been keeping for him. A chorus of cheerful good-byes, and with discarded coat and scarf under one arm and cardboard boxes and bags under the other, he makes his way to the parked car in the square.

Later in the day, suitably cleaned and polished, the morning's Bermondsey buys will reappear in the windows of antique shops dotted throughout London and the South of England.

The future of Bermondsey Market

Slowly, the New Caledonian is being forced to adapt itself to the general public, which is not only coming in greater numbers during the mid-morning, but is also becoming more noticeable in the early hours. The stallholders find themselves in a quandary. It is becoming increasingly difficult to find the quality goods to attract the regular specialist dealers, yet they are unwilling to follow the only inter-trading alternative, which is to supply the exporters with cheap bric-a-brac for bulk shipment to America and Italy. The middle way is in sale to private buyers; and if quality is to be preserved at Bermondsey, the stallholders will be forced into open encouragement of the general public.

Already some of the best buyers at Bermondsey are the Americans whose nose for good business so often brings them smartly to the action, wherever it may be. Rather unfairly the English antique trade tends to treat the Americans as 'easy game', and a stallholder may delight in frightening the poor Yankee tourist by mentioning a gigantic price for a cracked teapot that has been casually picked up from the stall and is, with a gasp, hurriedly replaced. In practice the experienced American collector is often more knowledgeable, more dedicated, and more particular about condition and quality than his European counterpart; indeed American taste and the confident financial backing of this taste are arguably the two most important influences on the contemporary antique trade. In Bermondsey middle-aged American couples, attended by a local carrier, wander slowly past the stalls carefully choosing items of certain quality that they are unable to find back home. No doubt many of these Americans with their own printed stickers and fluent private price code are in fact professional dealers, but their buying of small consignments of medium-range goods is a far more sympathetic operation than the English exporters' shipment of 250 cheap Edwardian barometers and 50 hall-stands in a single bulk container.

Change is inevitable, but it will be sad if the New Caledonian Market ever loses its extraordinary feeling of communal warmth. Many of us passers-by who are not even dealers, much less stallholders, can never appreciate fully the friendship and shared interest that unites the Bermondsey regulars, but even to outsiders awareness of this distinctive atmosphere brings a special satisfaction to Friday mornings. The other day the oldest Market Inspector of the New Caledonian retired and one of the last surviving founder-stallholders made a collection on his behalf; everyone in the market knew the two old-timers, and the visitors that morning had tangible proof of the long-standing tradition of comradeship that remains the backbone of the market. And although the old cockney families have been replaced by predominantly middle-class dealers, many of whom only work part-time in the trade, the individuality of the market is still protected; it is protected for the simple reason that many of the newcomers are drawn to Bermondsey because of these very qualities of freedom and friendliness which they do their utmost to preserve. Old life-styles disappear but the spirit of the past lives on at the New Caledonian.

A stallholder takes advantage of builders' hoardings near The Galleries in Camden Passage

3 Camden Passage

The character of Camden Passage

Foreign visitors making their way to the 'Angel' and from there along to Camden Passage are often surprised by their first sight of a London working-class High Street in full swing. The wide pavements are solid with the prams and children of young mothers going busily about their daily shopping, and there is a sense of haste and purpose that seldom reaches the casual freedom of West End shoppers. English visitors can enjoy the romance of street-names like Pentonville Road and Angel Islington which stood out at the slightly sinister bottom end of their Monopoly boards.

In fact the Angel is one of the few parts of Islington to have escaped radical redevelopment over the last few years, and the dainty smartness of Camden Passage is actually far more typical of present-day Islington than the busy High Street.

Quiet and orderly, Camden Passage is not only closed to all motor traffic but is also preserved entirely for trade in antiques, crafts and clothes. The Passage is therefore devoted to luxury trade with a prevailing atmosphere of relaxed and uncompetitive well-being, especially after lunch, which many of the dealers take in the renowned comfort of their local pub, the Camden Head. Throughout the day the numerous coffee-shops along the Passage are as busy and as business-like as the market stalls.

The sense of well-being communicated by the market people is matched by the setting, for practically without exception the shops and stalls in the market are newly painted, their ordered windows filled with appealing objects, and only the occasional stall of tangled bric-a-brac interrupts the vista of consistent smartness. Antique dealers as a race incline towards unconventionality and even shabbiness in appearance; Camden Passage comes as close to 'chic' as dealing can.

Camden Passage's smartness is more of necessity than choice, for although it has a long history of street trading, the area was severely bombed during the second world war and has been, indeed still is being, built up as a conscious 'antique' development. Every month new shops open and old shops are redesigned as the trading power of the Passage steadily increases. Even the stall sections of Camden Passage were constructed in phase with the proliferation of antique shops, and in contrast with the other markets described in this book, it is the shops and not the stalls that attract the most attention. The overwhelming impression of prosperity is completed by spiced and garlicked lunchtime smells from several delectable restaurants.

But despite its self-conscious creation Camden Passage has a genuine and distinctive charm. The tidy shops have an old-English, country-village look about them, and the people in the shops and on the stalls confirm the country image by appearing more interested in pleasure than profit. After all, the Passage is no longer than a village street, and after a month or two's trading newcomers can be on friendly terms with everyone in the market; this friendliness among the traders communicates itself to the visitors, who quickly feel themselves part of a natural communal activity. On sunny days the street is lined with contented dealers lounging in high-backed Victorian chairs, leaving their shops to take care of themselves.

On Saturdays these rural qualities are less evident as a crowd of determined tourists, week-end beer-drinkers making for the Camden Head, and an indigenous flock of quasi-hippies, all drift back and forth past nearly twice as many stalls as appear on any other day. Decked in this week-end finery of gay crowds and jumbled stalls Camden Passage suddenly seems a spontaneous street market, and that dreary haul up the Pentonville Road from Euston is fully justified. If supporters of the traditional markets still see all too clearly the tell-tale signs of conscious development, even on Saturdays, their doubts are not shared by the majority, who warm gladly to the imaginative displays and unhurried pace of the Passage.

Anyway, it is the people not the buildings that give character to any market, and Camden Passage has its fair share of amusing regulars. But more important even than the individuals is the over-all personality, and the stallholders and shopkeepers of Camden Passage share a determination to enjoy themselves at all costs. While many of the stallholders are in fact part-timers in the antique trade this pleasure-seeking attitude is in no way detrimental, for all the nicest and many of the best dealers in London look upon their work as a pleasurable pastime, and bring humour and imagination to the trade as a result. Outsiders often suspect the antique trade of overt commercialism and covert deception, when in fact many people who turn to dealing do so as an escape from these precise characteristics in other walks of life. Dealers are by and large a race of quiet individualists and enthusiastic amateurs, who enjoy equally their constant accumulation of knowledge and the unfettered friendships involved in their work. The Camden Passage dealers, many of them self-confessed amateurs, gloriously exemplify these uncommercial charms, despite the business-like organization of the market.

Much of this casual quality derives from the wide variety of individuals who frequent the market. Many of the dealers are involved outside their businesses in all sorts of creative ventures in the performing arts – at times

Two chefs from Carrier's Restaurant take the air at the Pierrepont Market

they seem like a colony of resting or retired artists – and this fullness of personality attracts the best of local support. On some days the Passage will be resplendent with the richly dyed, luxuriant curls of the stallholders' artistic friends, and the atmosphere of freedom and infectious excitement spills over to the unprepared tourist.

During the week, however, the mood of the market is most accurately represented in Terry's Tea Bar up above the Flea Market. Terry is a splendid Anglo-Italian woman whose broad shoulders and fiery eyes command instant submission from all but the hardiest males, and her maternal dictatorship extends far beyond the narrow confines of her formica counter. Terry's regulars provide her with a hot-line to market gossip, and nothing of significance can happen without Terry hearing and approving.

The rival snack counter and rendezvous is Natalie's Coffee Shop which fills the Athenai Arcade with a pleasant aroma of roasted coffee from its hide-out in the basement. The whole Athenai Arcade is fitted out in smart stripped pine, is pleasantly lighted and always beautifully warm, creating a protective snugness that suits both 'Natalie' and many of the stallholders. As Natalie's food is also delicious it is difficult to choose between her confined cosiness and Terry's insistent familiarity.

The proximity of the City brings business to four restaurants situated within a hundred yards of each other, and the mid-afternoon peace is often shattered by shouts of laughter from their burgundy-flushed clients. Carrier's is renowned for the French sophistication of its menu, while Frederick's is perhaps more reliable in its cuisine. But neither is cheap, and visitors who have left their expense accounts in the office may prefer to take lunch along with most of the stallholders at a 'real English pub', the Camden Head, whence acid-etched mirror glass and crimson velvet button upholstery set off the efficient service of 'bangers', shepherd's pie, macaroni and other traditional pub fare.

Only the most determined weight-watchers can resist the temptations to eat all along Camden Passage, but the calorie-conscious may find refuge in near-by Chapel Market where every day except Monday the barrow boys display an absolutely fresh selection of fruit, vegetables and even fish.

Although Camden Passage generates its own business and is therefore a self-sufficient unit, it benefits directly from the artistic community which has grown up in this part of Islington. Indeed the gaiety and creativeness of the antique scene in the Passage, with twice-yearly costume festivals spicing the daily communal flavour, cannot be fully understood in isolation from the other artistic activities of the area. For instance, the King's Head pub in Upper Street has excellent lunchtime and evening theatre in its back room. In the evening a charcoal grill supper is provided before the performance and as often as not, diners will find when the performance begins that their tables are actually on the stage. The small theatre company concentrates on intimate drama which takes full advantage of this physical closeness of player and audience.

Locals also appreciate an adventurous cinema management at The Screen, overlooking Islington Green, which frequently has London premières of avant-garde films; then down Essex Road the Little Angel Marionette Theatre at Dagmar Passage, Cross Street, has more affinities with puppet theatre in Prague than with anything in Western Europe.

On high days the Camden Passage regulars, both buyers and sellers, seem to conspire together to create a dazzling show in which the best fun is reserved for themselves and their friends. Even though we outsiders must sometimes stand on the fringe of things, it is nevertheless good to come across a community in which one senses so much genuine creativity and good humour.

Some specialists of interest

As mentioned earlier, the quality of Camden Passage arises from the individuality of the shops and small covered arcades rather than the street stalls. At the entrance to the Pierrepont, the first arcade to be built, Victoria's 'Corner Cupboard' has a charming cluttered interior of beaded face guards, wax-fruit compositions under sparkling glass domes, and all sorts of other Victorian relics. A large tabby cat suns itself in the window, and one expects some long-departed great-aunt to pop out at any moment from behind a cut-paperwork screen. Two establishments at the other end by the Flea Market attract then puzzle passers-by. During the long summer lunchtimes notices on the doors frequently direct all enquirers to the Camden Head, and visitors move off with their questions unanswered. But it is worth persevering, for 'Jubilee' offers an ever-changing feast of postcards, commemorative plates, pottery figures and other mementoes, while Greta Woolf next door keeps an amazing menagerie of dogs, bears and other animals, in the various materials and forms popular in the 19th century.

The Athenai Arcade is composed of rather mean little cubicles in which dealers struggle to contain both themselves and their wares, but down at the end is one of the most sympathetic commercial Art Deco stalls on any of the London markets. Just recently the proprietor, Dan Klein, has opened a shop called High Camp in Canonbury Place, N.1, so the full range of his taste needs to be sampled in both establishments, but stall No. 6 still holds its own. Like many Camden Passage stallholders Dan is only a part-time dealer – being a professional musician is his principal occupation – and the majority of goods he sells actually come from his own vast collection of twenties and thirties ephemera. As with many amateurs who begin dealing merely as an extension of their enjoyment in collecting, Dan Klein and his wife are extremely knowledgeable about their subject without being in the least critical of collectors less expert than themselves; indeed they are always delightfully helpful. At the same time their enthusiasm for Art Deco has not dulled their enjoyment of other things, and they have also formed an outstanding collection of Decalcomania, those 18th-century glass vases and plates decorated internally with cut-prints within painted borders.

American visitors should not miss a dealer on Upper Street, across the road from Camden Passage: Deane and Adams, 'Principal Colonial Suppliers'. There the saloon décor sets off all the paraphernalia of the Wild West, ranging from mementoes of Billy the Kid to stage-coach furnishings, with the occasional suit of medieval armour thrown in. Fire-arms are their speciality, but they usually have some exciting Frederic Remington bronzes of bucking broncos and Indian warriors – although buyers should be on their guard for modern casts which can occasionally slip beneath the

Both the stalls and the stallholders at Camden Passage give an impression of ordered gentility so different from the other street markets

Behind the hoardings rises another Camden Passage antiques development, but in the meantime stallholders seize the chance of a cheap pitch in the main thoroughfare

scrutiny even of these imaginative and generally extremely reliable dealers.

Hinton Hunt commands a central position at the junction of Camden Passage with Charlton Place, and a thoroughly absorbing half-hour can be spent inspecting his shelves of exquisite model soldiers, knights in armour, Zulu warriors and other historical figures. All the models are designed and made by the shop, and detailed booklets are supplied to collectors giving information on the variations of uniform and battle formation. For those of us brought up on William Britain's lead soldiers, it takes an effort to adjust to the adult quality and accuracy of Hinton Hunt's models, which have a far more artistic appeal.

The shop opposite in Charlton Place could hardly be a greater contrast. Both the shop and its owner are known simply as 'Chiu', and he and John Jesse in Kensington Church Street are among the leading European dealers in artist-made, non-commercial Art Deco. Chiu is Chinese, and people are surprisingly suspicious of his forsaking Ming purities for Europe's hot-house exaggerations of the 1920s, although the two periods have marked similarities in their reliance on radical stylization. This is one of those shops

It may be cliché but 'they don't make loo pulls like they used to'

in which appreciation of the style and quality of the proprietor is definitely bound up with enjoyment of the objects themselves, and somehow Chiu's expressive, happy and at the same time drawn face is an integral part of the ambience of the pottery, glass and all the other things that he sells. London's dealing world is divided between Art Deco fans who covet only Chiu's exotic collection of art objects, and the remainder who dislike Art Deco but are equally envious of his winter wardrobe of floor-length fur coats.

At the northern end of Camden Passage various building-projects bring relative chaos, but tucked in at the end is the Orange Box which sells an enchanting collection of Victorian, Edwardian and later costume. The management is cheerfully unprofessional in attitude but none the less efficient and competitive in its purchasing, for there is a constant supply of unusual and attractive period clothes. Near by, the proprietors of Marbles, alias 'the Victorian Trading Company', have an equally cheerful outlook and make no effort to pretend that many of their pub mirrors and tobacco jars have any real age; indeed they happily discuss the merits of various methods of transfer-printing and painting these modern copies.

The general dealers in furniture and allied works of art in Camden Passage maintain a remarkably high standard and all are worth a visit. Some, however, are outstanding, and most London auction-goers sooner or later come across the name of Peter Hone, especially those searching for four-poster beds, the best of which always seem to end up with him. The marvellous thing about Hone's shop is that it seldom contains a single object that could be described as ordinary or straightforward. Many dealers with a distinctive taste usually find that they are forced to stock a number of good but standard pieces just through commercial expediency; but Peter Hone will have none of this and only sells furniture that appeals to him personally. Beds are his speciality, and his shop is the showcase for a continuous parade of extravagant bedroom fortresses, as well as some magnificent tapestry hangings that soften the sculptural excess of his Baroque taste. The strangest variety of objects appeal to Hone, and the quickly changing shop window may accommodate, in the space of a week, items as varied as a gigantic cast-iron stove, an exquisite 17th-century Japanese lacquer screen, a pair of grotesque Victorian nubian torchères and a rare set of French Empire gilt-wood dining chairs.

It is fascinating to see how quickly the most talented dealers establish a flourishing trade. Vieux-Pernon's shop has been one of the relatively recent successes. His Hermitage Antiques, almost opposite Peter Hone, has improved each week from the day of opening. But just as important as the actual furniture is the tone of its presentation. Margaret Deighton, just round the corner, also possesses this enviable ability of creating an agreeable ambience.

But Camden Passage is full of such delights, and visitors should look around carefully for shops and stalls that appeal to their own personal tastes.

Finally, walking back towards the Angel, connoisseurs can seldom just pass by the best Victorian public lavatory in north London. Unfortunately its palatial comforts are threatened with destruction to make way for road-building, and before long its colourful ceramic tiles and bold brasswork will themselves be appearing on the stalls of Camden Passage; the most coveted mementoes will be the elaborate manufacturer's plaques on which Doulton proudly present their native town of Paisley on equal terms with Paris and London.

Some years ago an illustrious attendant kept his goldfish in the original glass tanks above the urinals. The fish lived to a ripe old age in these ideal conditions, a grill protecting them from an unhappy descent while their water was constantly changed. The Islington community can be expected to preserve Camden Passage and its companion facilities with equal individuality for many years to come.

The future of Camden Passage

Until the last war Camden Passage was well known to music-hall enthusiasts who passed through on their way to Collins's at the end of Islington Green, there to enjoy the luxury of a wicker seat in one of the boxes for a few shillings. At the turn of the century Kate Carney had been a regular at Collins's, and she used to take the young Charlie Chaplin across the Green to amuse himself at the Victorian Toy Shop on the present site of The Galleries at the end of Camden Passage.

The new development of Camden Passage as a centre for antiques is largely the personal achievement of one John Friend and his associates, whose enthusiasm and paternal management created and now controls the major part of the market. In 1960, when Mr Friend laid the concrete and erected the awnings for the Pierrepont and Charlton Markets, the whole of Camden Passage was scheduled for residential redevelopment by the Council, and Leigh Underhill was the only antique dealer already in residence. But by the early 1960s the great surge of public interest in antique collecting was just beginning, and the market venture proved an immediate success. Money was raised for the Camden Passage Group of Companies and, as other independent dealers and the restaurateurs moved in, the Passage was saved from the Borough's demolition teams.

At the time of writing several important premises in Camden Passage are still in the process of redesign, and the final outlook and mood of the market are still by no means decided. An exciting future is planned for the large Victorian warehouse at the northern end of the Passage which will be called The Galleries, and will house on the ground floor a number of small shops all specially designed in the Regency style with attractive bow fronts. Two other floors are intended for adventurous exhibitions combined with sales of painting and furniture. The other major plan is the construction of an arcade in horseshoe shape on a site facing the Camden Head pub, linking the busy High Street and the quiet Passage. Down by the Pierrepont Arcade two old buildings are being completely redesigned and will provide further facilities. The last and most exciting project has yet to receive official sanction for it involves taking over the disused tram power-house at the Angel end of the market, a visually dramatic building constructed above one of the London plague pits.

It remains to be seen what will be made of all these interesting developments as the close attention of many companies suggests that Camden Passage has long commercial legs. However, on the open-market side of things the pattern for the future is already clearly defined, for the established general trading days Wednesdays and Saturdays are being augmented by different markets through the week: jewellery on Monday, furniture on Tuesday, contemporary art on Thursday, books on Friday. Only the jewellery day can be considered an immediate success, but John Friend's enthusiasm will doubtless conquer all obstacles in the end, and one would certainly expect his Friday book market gradually to replace the near-by Farringdon Road bookstalls, now a shadow of their pre-war glory. No doubt an excuse will soon be found to open the Passage and markets on a Sunday as well.

Although John Friend would be the first to say that the stallholders and shopkeepers themselves give the market its continuing character, few regulars would deny the value of his surveillance of the scene from his office in Phelps Cottage, in Upper Street. All the open stalls and a number of the indoor markets come directly under his supervision, and because of his kindly appearance he has astonished many trouble-making stallholders with the speed of their dismissal. His influence will remain to safeguard the contentment of regular stallholders as well as the ease and friendliness of the general atmosphere.

Traders learn the ropes at an early age in the East End markets (Cheshire Street)

4 The East End Markets

Cutler Street Silver Market

For the dedicated collector of silver and jewellery it's an early start in London on Sunday as well as Friday and Saturday, if there is to be any chance of beating the professionals to discoveries on the Cutler Street Market. This tiny specialized market, operating on Sunday mornings in Exchange Buildings Yard, off Cutler Street, sees some of the most active silver dealing in the whole of London, and private collectors will never regret the effort involved in becoming known and accepted in this fiercely competitive dealers' market.

For the uninitiated there is a slightly sinister atmosphere as early arrivals turn in from Houndsditch between the high windowless walls that line the narrow Cutler Street. At first there is no hint of the actual market; all that can be seen are small groups of dealers, with their coat collars turned up against the cold and their trilby hats well pulled down over their eyes. Occasionally a snappily dressed lady dealer or even some youngsters arrive early, but their behaviour is little different from the rest. Then, as if at a pre-arranged signal, the groups quietly break up, folding tables appear from a concealed door at the bottom end of the dark yard of Exchange Buildings, and the market is under way.

Soon after 8 o'clock the yard will be complete with lines of stalls at which the dealers unpack from their battered suitcases an assortment of silver, jewellery, coins, medals and even stamps. It is never quite clear exactly where all these people suddenly come from, as very few cars are ever parked in Cutler Street itself, and the majority just arrive quietly from all directions on foot, carrying their valuable stock in bags and cases. Occasionally, as on the Portobello, a dealer will be stopped by a friend, and business will be done there and then from the boot of a car, or kneeling on the pavement in front of an opened case. But even on the stalls themselves it is obvious that most of the buyers and sellers are well known to each other, and there is even an established order of seniority which gives certain dealers authority and preference over others. The conduct of business is extremely quiet and orderly, and there is little opportunity for a private buyer even to see, much less to buy any of the interesting items. For although the stalls themselves are all fairly full, a regular customer will hardly look at the open display when asking the stallholder, 'Anything for me, Ted?' At this, Ted may reach into his breast pocket and guardedly hand over half a dozen 16th-century apostle spoons for his friend's private inspection, while another client is offered a bundle of gold watch-chains from a coat pocket. It is even difficult to see much actual exchanging of money, but the volume of business is indicated by the occasional glimpse of a thick wad of twenty-pound notes disappearing into a well-used wallet.

The only sign of urgency in the Cutler Street Market is at the opening-time of the Baldacci Café on the corner, when a group of jewellery dealers make a determined dash for a table in the far corner, and Hebrew heads are bent over rings and bangles for careful inspection. Other dealers come and go from this busy table, but it is quite impossible for an outsider to partici-pate, and even while queuing for a coffee the private collector may feel like an intruder. The regulars themselves sometimes have difficulty making their way, for friends frequently fall out in this harsh dealing world of the silver boys. A smart-looking dealer asks one of the stallholders in the normal way if there is anything for him, and on being met with studied deafness, asks again, 'Come on, Bill, you know what I like.' 'Yeh, and I like it too, mate,' says Bill with a chilly smile, and goes on ignoring his erstwhile friend.

In practice it is always far less difficult than it first appears to make a mark in a strange place, and the stallholder only prefers to attend to another dealer because it is certain he is basically interested in buying. When a private collector has proved to the dealers that he also has the knowledge and keenness to buy with equal expertise, then Cutler Street will happily accept his custom.

From Cheshire Street to Petticoat Lane

Cutler Street is located just off Petticoat Lane (or Middlesex Street, as it is now known officially), and this, of course, is one of the favourite Sunday attractions for tourists in London. But unless they are first going to the silver market, Petticoat Lane visitors with a general interest in anti-ques and bric-a-brac should really start their inspection of the East End markets at the northern end, in Cheshire Street, which is the only place in these extensive markets with a substantial display of second-hand articles as opposed to the new goods of Petticoat Lane.

The whole of this area of London right down to the river at Wapping has been scheduled for redevelopment ever since the end of the war, when heavy bombing destroyed so many buildings. But although few East-Enders still live in these battered houses nothing much has happened in the way of rebuilding. Hoardings appear from time to time and streets are occasionally closed off, and the street markets have been forced to move

In the East End markets a good second-hand radio is far more inviting to most regulars than the pair of Victorian decanters displayed on the table in the foreground (Cheshire Street)

about at the bidding of the local Council who grant the licences. The Cheshire Street Market, in fact, used to be held in Vallance Road, which was far better known by name to Londoners as a hunting ground for cheap second-hand furniture and furnishings.

Approaching the markets from Whitechapel or Bethnal Green on a Sunday morning, the first sign of activity begins near the crossing of Cheshire Street with Vallance Road. Initially the scene is saddening, as rows of old men in tattered clothes lay out their most respectable belongings on the pavement, in the hope that someone slightly less poor than themselves may give them a few pence for an old tie or an empty biscuit tin. But only too soon the visitor's sympathy is forgotten in the excitement of the milling crowd of East-Enders, full of life and fun.

The largest conglomeration of likely stalls is administered by I. Ratzker and Sons, 'Rag, Woollen and Metal Merchants', through and behind whose premises runs a bewildering maze of stalls. In terms of antique collecting the best things available are books, clothes, pottery oddments, and desk ornaments, but almost anything can turn up. 'Dinky Toy' collectors – and they do exist – congregate at a specialist stall, but collectors of a more practical bent will be interested in the sets of battered but highly repairable balloon-back chairs, and useful oddments like coal scuttles or those efficient wooden shoe-trees that nobody makes any longer.

Although one occasionally recognizes a Portobello stallholder filling her bags with odds and ends to stock next Saturday's stall, Cheshire Street functions primarily for the locals and not the visitors. Second-hand television sets, washing machines, saucepans, tool kits and other cheap, usable goods are naturally of more interest to the majority of shoppers than porcelain dishes. More important than anything else, however, are the second-hand clothes which save these housewives from the impossible expense of clothing their large families with new dresses and suits, for a little altering and repairing quickly restore some marvellous clothes to wearability. In one particular building the long tables are piled high with old clothes and hundreds more coats, dresses and trousers hang from the rafters. Here hippies compete with the locals for some tremendous bargains. 'A pound for a suit of clothes' is a familiar cry down Cheshire Street, and the hand-stitched lapels and torn tailor's labels reveal the fashionable Savile Row origins of many suits for sale.

Walking westwards towards Sclater Street, the crowds become even thicker, and although the houses are still battered and boarded, many more of the shops are still in business. There is J. W. Agass at No. 20 Cheshire Street doing a roaring trade in aquarium fish, and his stall on the street outside the shop does equally well with tortoises and grass snakes. C. and K. Televisions claim to supply the cheapest guaranteed sets in London, and a constant stream of cockney kids flow into the 'mod' clothes and shoe shops which allow them to dress fashionably at half the price of Chelsea boutiques.

By the time Cheshire Street crosses Brick Lane and becomes Sclater Street the second-hand goods stalls have been replaced by stalls selling fruit, tinned food, kitchen utensils and other household effects. Again everything is reduced in price and the stallholders all have their individual 'patter'. The crockery-sellers are the most exciting, shouting out the gradual reductions in price of whole tea-sets which they persist in throwing high in the air to be caught with a tremendous clatter on a tin tray. The best trade, however, is done on the tinned foodstuffs on which thrifty housewives save for family holidays from their meagre budget. Everything is miraculously cheap, oranges at eight for ten pence, kitchen knives at twenty pence; in desperation one morning the knife-seller offered to dispose of his stall and all the stock for only thirty pounds!

Having walked this far, visitors should certainly push their way to the end of Sclater Street towards the sound of yelping puppies and screeching birds. Although all this is strictly beyond the limit of 'antique' markets, collectors of antiques will surely appreciate the traditional qualities of the famous Club Row pet market, which has found a new home here across the road on Sclater Street. Little has changed since the 1920s when the modeller Charles Vyse was making studies for market figures in pottery (page 98); and the cry still goes up, 'Here's a good 'un!' One of the dog-sellers specializes in Chow puppies which charge about their deep straw box rebounding off one another; it is hardly surprising that so many onlookers refuse to believe that these lively animals are liable to infection, as pet-shop owners would have it.

Dozens of children hang over the edges of the hamster and puppy boxes, but Club Row is not entirely for the children. The tall house at No. 1 Sclater Street advertises 'Livestock Upstairs', and is well known to aviary enthusiasts for the quality and variety of its exotic birds. These second-floor premises are lined with spotlessly clean cages full of humming birds, para-keets and many other breeds. There is even a toucan or two, and turkey chicks. Another favourite hobby of East-Enders is keeping tropical fish, and there are several excellent stalls beside the railway line; while other stalls specialize in the animal foodstuffs.

From Club Row, market-goers generally make their way back towards Liverpool Street Station *via* Commercial Street, which gives them a view of Hawksmoor's dilapidated but magnificent Christchurch and All Saints, the Parish Church of Spitalfields. A sharp right turn past Spital-fields Market leads into the Petticoat Lane Market itself, with its host of persuasive sellers of knock-down modern goods. People familiar with this colourful market before the war miss some of the old quacks like Conrad the Corn King, who claimed to have cured half the crowned heads of Europe with his patent medicine, but there are still plenty of attractions. It is beyond comprehension how stallholders can make a profit, much less a living, selling waterproof, shock-proof, self-winding Swiss watches with a year's guarantee for only £2·50 each; most tourists assume that the watches are stolen and walk away shaking their heads, although the stallholders normally display in all honesty both their names and numbered Stepney Street Trading Licences. The sellers of cheap trinkets, on the other hand, actually imply that their goods are stolen, although this may only be to make the prices sound more credible. As the hawker sorts out bags of gold trinkets his patter runs something like this: 'And now, ladies and gentle-men, not for £8, not for £6, not for £4, not for £2, but to the fella' wot 'as the sensibility to recognize a bargain, only £1 – and quick 'cos when the man in blue strolls d'an that way, me and mi box o' bangles will be orf t'other way at fifty miles an hour. You couldn't buy stolen goods cheaper, and these ain't stolen, they, 'ow shall I put it, just ain't been paid for.' Round the corner a couple of twelve-year-old cockney kids knock out their barrow-load of skirts and blouses with a fluent patter that only comes from the experience of generations.

Petticoat Lane, recently renamed Middlesex Street, looks almost as new as its name. But in the adjoining streets the market scene has changed little since Mayhew's time a century ago. There are still secluded covered markets where East-Enders sell piles of old clothes by Dutch auction for as little as 1p and never more than 20p; and the Bell Lane Poultry Market still opens its doors on a Sunday morning for a flourishing trade in hens, chickens and cockerels, which are chosen in their pens and killed on the spot.

Many pessimists claim that London is losing all its traditional character beneath a mass of rebuilding, and that the street trader is being forced to the wall by the economic necessity of large-scale retailing. But visitors to the East End markets on a Sunday morning, especially in Cheshire and Sclater Streets, will see for themselves that market life is still full of vigour. There are sad sights of crippling poverty, and the houses are often boarded and bare, but the stalls and the stallholders are brimming over with cockney enthusiasm; even those visitors with eyes only for 'antiques' will enjoy their walk through Cheshire Street to Club Row and on to Liverpool Street.

5 The smaller markets

Church Street and Bell Street Markets, Lisson Grove

The market in Church Street on Saturdays fulfils the same function for this part of London as Sclater Street for East-Enders, that is to say, it provides cheap food and commodity shopping. Church Street is of interest to us here because of the cluster of antique stalls and arcades near Lisson Grove, and, perhaps more significantly, for the junk market at the Edgware Road end of the parallel Bell Street.

Compared with the Portobello Road Market which also runs on Saturdays, Church Street Market has few antiques, but if collectors should find themselves in the area it is well worth a visit, as its prices tend to be considerably lower than its more popular rivals'. Its star attraction is a small covered arcade at the end, called the Courtyard, whose pillar-box-red stalls are pleasantly stocked. The Merda Antique Market and the Antique Bazaar also have possibilities, and there are a couple of good stalls for second-hand books and Victorian chairs. Church Street can also boast an Oriental carpet stall which far outclasses anything on the Portobello; not only is the stall itself groaning under the weight of carpets, but Persian rugs and colourful Kelims are laid out all over the road as well.

Walking down Lisson Grove towards Marylebone one passes Phillips' auction rooms, where the Friday sales are well worth attending for cheap house furnishing. Phillips' main auctions rooms are in Blenheim Street, off Bond Street, and only the very lowest grade of antiques are sent for sale in these Marylebone rooms; but a surprising number of West End dealers attend the sales, so things of interest must turn up from time to time. Bell Street itself leads off on the right further down Lisson Grove and is one of the favourite haunts of second-hand book collectors, there being several charming old-fashioned bookshops to be found; the best is Greer Books at No. 87. At the other end of the street, approaching Edgware Road, dedicated bargain-hunters will enjoy checking through a number of junk stalls that line the pavement on both sides. Some stallholders in Bell Street manfully struggle to raise the standard of goods displayed, but this remains basically a true junk market, which, in these days of fashionable pretensions for 'antiques', is a mark of distinction.

Finding the smaller antique street markets

Despite the pressures of a changing world, the old street markets of London are still surprisingly numerous; an enquiry at the local Town Hall about licences for street trading gives some indication of the amazing number of stallholders still earning a living on the streets. Almost all these general markets will have a stall or two selling second-hand goods of one sort or another.

Collectors living in London should spend some time searching through their immediate localities. For example residents of Kennington, Walworth and the surrounding area south of the river should keep an eye on the Sunday market in Westmoreland Road, where all sorts of interesting things can be found. Then there are old markets, like the Cut at Waterloo, which have passed away completely but may suddenly come to life again; and once famous but now narrowly surviving markets like the book market in Farringdon Road, where half a dozen stalls do business between 11.30 a.m. and 2.30 p.m. on Monday to Friday.

In addition London collectors have a choice of all the covered antique markets which have become so popular, and these have stalls similar to those in and around the street markets described in this book. Some of these private markets, like that run by the Royal Standard in Vanburgh Park, Blackheath, are even conducted in the open air, which might be thought to qualify them for detailed attention in this book. But I have chosen to limit discussion entirely to those markets whose character and quality is defined by the predominance of actual street selling.

In the following chapters we shall look at the practical business of collecting antiques, and how the markets can be used to the best advantage.

This 'harvest putto' is one of a pair of book-ends produced by the Ashtead Pottery between 1926 and 1935. Purchased on the Portobello at £14 the pair in summer 1973, this is a bargain by any standards

Part Two: Collecting in the Markets

6 Collecting trends

Ten years ago, one of the established London dealers could walk down the Portobello Road on a Saturday morning and expect to pick up three or four pieces of 18th-century porcelain at under £20 each. Today the same dealer competes with crowds twenty times the size, and would be delighted to find just one similar piece at under £200. It is hardly surprising that the older dealers lament the passing of those halcyon days when today's rarities were part of daily dealing, and bargains abounded at every country sale and market stall.

Indeed the speed of developments in the antique trade has left its casualties, since many dealers have been unable to adjust to cope with either the mass of new objects receiving the attention of collectors or the aggressive new public interest in the whole collecting scene. But, because so many more people are now involved in both dealing and collecting, the whole scope of the trade has expanded in a way that can only be to the good. Although many older collectors find themselves priced out of the market, and their dealer friends now handle objects previously condemned as valueless junk, the best from both sides readily admit that the world of 'antiques' is more imaginative, more colourful, and far more exciting than it used to be.

The gigantic expansion of the antique trade over the last decade has penetrated to all levels of this previously staid and stratified world. No longer can London's West End dealers dare to conduct their businesses on the assumption that the knowledge and possession of works of art are forever confined to a gloved handful of their intimate friends and acquaintances. In order to survive in a fiercely competitive world, successful 'antique' businesses have had to develop their own brand of gentlemanly commercialism. The 'magnates' of Christie's and Sotheby's, who used to guard their secrets as though the safety of the nation were at stake, now eagerly draw the attention of television directors to all the esoteric goings-on in the London auction houses. Only a few stalwart members of these firms openly mourn the invasion of their sanctums, as the television crews close in on the satin-voiced consummation of their auction rites.

At this level, the general expansion of the market has been accompanied by a shattering series of record auction prices. Nowadays, sales-clerks can frequently be seen escorting elderly owners to easy chairs where the news can be gently broken that their family punch-bowl has just secured several thousand pounds, when the highest conceivable valuation before the sale had been no more than a few hundred. Sadly, there is some reason to believe that the astronomical prices reached in certain areas are the direct result of injections of speculative money from big institutional investors. So far, these speculators are accompanied by an even greater number of new private collectors whose purchases are not directly motivated by considerations of profit, and this still protects the art market from fluctuating in the same manner as the London Stock Exchange and other money-markets.

But all this buying and selling of single objects each worth thousands or even millions of pounds remains remote from the wide collecting public, many of whom understandably believe that only people with five-figure deposit accounts are admitted beneath the portals of Christie's. Indeed despite the publicity given to the London sale-rooms, business is still conducted among a relatively small group of people, and almost 85 per cent of the purchases are made by dealers. Because of the enormous prices and esoteric machinations of the West End, the vast new collecting public has impinged most directly at less exalted levels of the antique trade, and principally on the street markets.

Indeed it is in the antique street markets that the most imaginative advances in the trade are currently being made. The visual and practical pleasures described earlier in this book do much to explain the popularity of the markets, but their success can also be seen in the wider context of changing social attitudes.

Without stretching generalization too far it is possible to find links between the collecting boom and the post-war liberation of taste and ideas in many other fields. The rehabilitation of grandma's glasses, the 'Gay is Good' campaign, light shows, wide colourful ties on City gents, the second-hand-clothes look in Chelsea boutiques, the new styling of men's hair, and many other aspects of modern living all have an imaginative visual basis for their appeal that would have been meaningless ten years ago. And just as society was becoming more visually aware of its surroundings, the full ecological horror of industrial progress received broad publicity, and one of the natural reactions to its threat has been a turning back of people's attention to the arts and artifacts of the recent and not-so-recent past.

Obviously the desire of a new generation to decorate both itself and its homes with amusing, even elegant, Edwardian bric-a-brac does not on its own explain the Portobello phenomenon; it is just one example of the new visual acquisitiveness which is the sociological root of the broadening of collecting interest.

But whatever the underlying causes, it will be apparent to even the most casual observer that since about 1968 the street markets have enjoyed a remarkable surge of commercial power. Success was due at first to their imaginative response to the demands of foreign tourists, and then to the continuing energy of the stallholders in ferreting out new delights for the expanding home trade. Moreover, the market business is supported by numerous background figures, including characters as diverse as the property or shipping investors who provide the capital and the 'totters' and 'knockers' who supply the bulk of the goods, and it was their joint appreciation of the commercial possibilities of the paraphernalia of the Victorian and Edwardian past that made the market boom a reality. Suddenly, three or four years ago, the shops and stalls on the markets blossomed with enticing displays of colourful curiosities, mad memorabilia and a host of forgotten arts with previously unknown decorative and collecting qualities. The public gladly joined in the creation of new collecting fields, until now, informed by the media and encouraged by recent fashions in interior design, vast new sections of the community devote time and money to collecting.

Of course all this has led to certain price exaggerations and collecting absurdities, but the opening up of new interests should afford nothing but delight to those with a real feeling for the antique trade. Collecting used to be largely the prerogative of the carriage-trade rich, under the tutelage of West End dealers, who first selected their clients' paintings or pots and then initiated them in the correct aesthetic responses. Now one may see a London typist deliberating agonizingly over the purchase of a super twenties coffee-set from a Saturday afternoon Camden stall, where a couple of years ago the same girl would have strongly resisted possessing anything more than six months old, amid the fashion for throw-away modernity.

This broadening of the street-market scene has produced some rapid translations from street-stall bargain to top-price lot at a Christie's sale. It has become possible literally to make a fortune within a year or two by forming a substantial collection of a neglected field just before it reaches the attention of wealthy West End dealers. The problem is to foresee the course of fashion, and some of the developments, like £1,000 Fairings, are so unpredictable by rational means that dealers have been known to consult the occult. But although there are now so many people on the track of these shooting stars, there will always be scope on the markets for someone of independent taste to create, at minimal cost, a collection that in years to come will be recognized for its artistic and historical qualities. People who claim to be in the know may say that there is nothing 'good' to be found in the street markets any more, but these false philosophers were probably saying the same thing ten years ago when they lacked the imagination to see the qualities of Art Nouveau, Japanese ivories, Victorian paintings and all the other recent 'flyers'. For whether it be the luck in liking it or the skill in recognizing it, for the discerning there is always quality lurking among the rubbish that first fills the eye at most markets, and the thrill of collecting against fashion is far more real and personal in eagle-eyed excursions down the Portobello Road than from a gilded seat at Sotheby's sales.

The stories of discoveries on the markets are legion, and one or two of these are told elsewhere in this book. As one might expect, the best finds are usually made by professionals, and although fewer and fewer period objects appear on the stalls of the London markets, knowledgeable dealers and collectors still comb the larger markets every week, from time to time spotting the finest Shibuichi Tsuba, Clichy paperweight, Novgorod icon or some other rarity. However, of far greater general interest than these exotic treasures are the things of quality that remain relatively cheap because only very few people have responded to the attractions of the subject. For instance, fifteen years ago a limited number of discerning collectors succeeded magnificently in picking out the most exciting examples of Art Nouveau and Art Deco glass, and there was always the chance to buy one of those 'dreadful Tiffany lamps' for a small sum. Now the best sell for several thousand pounds.

Since Tiffany wisteria lamps are now so popular, people are tempted to argue that there is nothing in the markets of that kind of quality still unknown to the collecting public. Yet there are many more recent examples which would suggest the contrary. Four years ago the names of William de Morgan, Christopher Dresser and Charles Cundall would have meant little to the average Portobello stallholder, and none of them would have believed that demand for 19th-century Studio Pottery could so soon justify Judy Fox opening a shop specializing in it entirely. During the three-year period 1970–73 several factors influenced this change of taste, in particular the sharp rise in prices of 18th-century ceramics, and the creation by Sotheby's of an auction house in Belgravia devoted exclusively to the arts of the period 1830 to 1930. During these last three years prices for most Studio Pottery have risen from a gratefully received £10 to an easy £60, and the best examples have suddenly become worth as much as several hundred or even a thousand pounds. No doubt the whole subject will soon disappear over the modest collector's horizon to join Tiffany lamps in the boudoirs of the rich.

If Studio Pottery has already joined the ranks of missed opportunities, perhaps hope can be nurtured by a more recent example. Quite unexpectedly in late April 1973 a sale at Sotheby's Belgravia recorded unprecedented prices for late 19th-century Japanese lacquer and Shibayama, and a

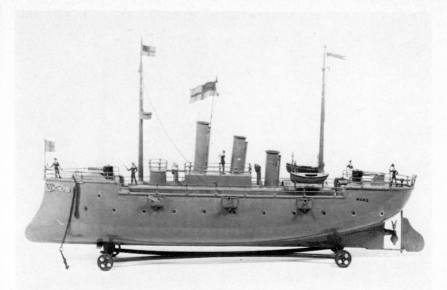

Two painted tin clockwork toys, produced in Germany between 1900 and 1915. These are avidly sought after by collectors

Photographic equipment is rapidly increasing in value and these large phenakistoscope discs are highly sought after

Sotheby's regular who had left a miniature lacquer cabinet for which he had previously been unable to find a buyer at £60, could scarcely believe his ears when it was sold for £750. Almost overnight, long-time collectors of late Japanese lacquer found themselves worth a small fortune, all through trusting their own judgement against prevailing taste and thus finding things of quality unheeded on market stalls.

In retrospect, reasons could be found for this dramatic auction result. Interest in the subject had been building up for some time in both Japan and France, and the mounting of a specialized sale containing many outstanding lots inevitably attracted competitive bidding from all over the world. However, the explanation did not lessen the impact on private collectors, who for years had been used to a free hand on the markets.

The real 'find' has nowadays become an increasing rarity, partly because press and television coverage of antiques and collecting has led many people to appreciate, and in some cases overvalue their possessions. Yet even now good luck can come anyone's way. A church fête recently yielded a pleasant oil-painting of a harvest scene which was offered at only £1·25. Bought hesitantly and half-heartedly rubbed with a damp cloth to reveal the signature, it was soon afterwards sold at auction for £700. Finds like this always happen to someone else; but it is encouraging to hear that at least they still happen.

Chance windfalls are immensely exciting, but the greatest personal satisfaction in collecting has always been found in exploring neglected fields, and for this pursuit the street markets are ideal. Indeed the most remarkable story of private pioneer collecting in post-war years is centred round the Portobello Road; for it was here that Charles and Lavinia Handley-Read found many of the finest pieces in their collection of Victorian decorative arts. The Handley-Read's intense dedication to the subject they adopted together in the early 1950s resulted in the formation of a collection that earned a Royal Academy Exhibition in Easter 1972, and later passed in its entirety into the national collections. The story has a tragic ending, for his subject became a destructive obsession for Handley-Read. His meticulous notes on the collection and indeed the collection itself began to appear totally inadequate to him as the time of the exhibition approached. Finally, a few months before the opening of the exhibition which in the event received universal acclaim, he committed suicide, followed a fortnight later by his wife.

Although the climax was tragic, Charles Handley-Read's articles in *The Times* and elsewhere had described his happiness in collecting on the Portobello, and many of the unusual pieces in the collection bore labels telling of their discovery in dark corners of the markets. One of the most interesting finds was the Gothic Revival dining-room suite which 'the

Portobello Road again provided', at a price of '£18 the lot'; unfortunately the suite was split up, a serving table going to the Victoria and Albert Museum while the dining table was sold at Sotheby's Belgravia for £520, and later found its way to Mallett's the Bond Street dealers at an asking price over £1,000.

Despite the recent commercialization of 'Victoriana' there are still many neglected areas in the field of 19th-century decorative arts, some of which, along with the more amusing curiosities of the period, are suggested in the section which follows.

7 The pleasures of collecting

At times, notably on wet November days when beset on all sides by rising prices, the most devoted market visitor will question whether the whole business of 'collecting' really is as pleasurable as he had imagined. On a bad day the crowded Portobello scene can stir up an instinctive antagonism to the ugly materialism of a 'collecting' society, intensified on closer inspection of the quality of the mass of goods being offered for sale. Such reactions are understandable, but they arise from a failure to appreciate that most London markets cater for the kind of customer who comes for a specific purpose, not for those who are expecting to be seduced into a purchase by artistic display and smooth salesmanship. The essential character of the markets is precisely this uninhibited display of masses of material, the majority of which neither is nor pretends to be anything more than junk.

In order to avoid disappointment in the apparent profusion of meaningless bric-a-brac it is essential to come to the markets in search of something particular, even if that something is no more than the sight of colourful characters, or some unusual birthday present or memento.

Indeed the markets will satisfy many needs, but they give their best to the small collector who returns week after week in search of pieces for his developing collection. It matters not at all what the object of enchantment is, for the arousing of a genuine passion for any collectable item will at once invest the stalls of previously colourless odds and ends with unlimited possibilities and interest. It is extraordinary the way a collector will instantly see through the mass of bric-a-brac to the objects that have meaning for his experienced eyes; things that will even attract a non-collecting companion once they have been pointed out.

The majority of regulars at the markets are motivated by this genuine attraction to the objects themselves, but they are also accompanied by those creatures of fashion who now collect merely for collecting's sake, ever since it became apparent that the name Chippendale could be dropped with even greater success than the Aga Khan's. Seldom can a fashion have been dutifully followed with more unexpected reward of pleasure than that of collecting.

The first enjoyment of collecting is of course the quest; next comes the pride and pleasure of simple possession. Indeed the true collector savours more than anything else the days he spends on his own, just carefully cleaning and repairing, sorting and resorting the ever-growing number of objects that form his collection.

For some there can also be considerable intellectual satisfaction in collecting, and the expertise of many private enthusiasts quickly outstrips the professionals in the more obscure fields. Indeed there are certain subjects, such as early photography, where the real experts are all private collectors, because in those fields which are largely unresearched in any depth the only way of acquiring detailed information is through the practical experience of collecting. It is easy enough to gain a passing familiarity with a subject by reading through some well-illustrated modern monograph, but this kind of knowledge is worthless compared with detailed information that a collector will acquire through collating and comparing the variations and rarities he finds in his collecting forages. At the same time the practised market-goer develops a sixth sense for unearthing documentary material concerning his subject, whether this new evidence is to be found in contemporary periodicals lying around on bookstalls, or in connection with the history of a completely different field. The absolute determination of most collectors to find out everything there is to know about the things in their possession also leads to dedicated research in museums and libraries; and so first-rate expertise quickly builds up in various ways.

However, the collector's life is not without its dangers, for a pleasurable pastime can grow monstrously into an incurable disease, affecting job, family, holidays, bank balance and almost anything else you care to mention. It all begins innocently enough with the purchase of an odd plate now and then, but casual interest soon becomes passionate involvement, and a year or two later cups begin to have an attraction too, the new 'affaire' taking a vice-like grip even before the awareness of its existence has fully dawned. Indeed every collector must, at some stage, feel his sanity threatened by the virulence of the collecting fever, especially when handing £20 in cash without hesitation to a stallholder the same day the Bank Manager has threatened instant destruction for further indebtedness.

The emphasis chosen for a particular collection is largely a matter of individual temperament, for there are countless alternatives. Some collectors aim to re-create a complete picture of a particular historical period and will gather about themselves all sorts of artistic and domestic artifacts from that age, while others narrow this period interest down to objects that have a specific and limited style, like Art Nouveau. Another kind of collecting zeal expresses itself in concentration on examples of a particular object, say tobacco-stoppers, from all periods and in all media, whereas others confine their interest to a particular medium, glass for example, but will consider every kind of object in that medium. Others again give no emphasis at all to their buying, collecting everything and anything purely on its decorative qualities; it is astonishing how certain people have an innate ability to make marvellous decorative use of bits and pieces which most collectors would regard as junk. All the same it is sometimes quite impossible to understand the evident enthusiasm with which some purchases are made, and observers must never rule out the possibility that they are witnessing the author Bevis Hillier gloating over the acquisition of another horror to swell his private Museum of Bad Taste, which already contains a gruesome menagerie of stuffed frogs dancing beneath glass domes.

If the items of potential collectable interest are numberless, so the character of Collecting Man defies categorization, ranging from the self-effacing postcard collector meeting his colleagues for convivial evenings at the local Church Hall, to the monocled barrister pursuing his lone quest for jewelled seals and fobs. Although there is no external uniformity there are certain character patterns as well as natural antipathies among the market regulars. For example the early record collector, with an operatic glint in his eye and the hint of two-step in his gait, while nodding sympathetically to a mezzo-tint buff, will deliberately ignore the sharp-eyed collector of Georgian spoons.

Cigarette-card collectors are perhaps the most remarkable of the gregarious breed, for they all rely heavily on their privately-printed trade magazine, *The Cigarette Card News and Trade Card Chronicle*, and their central organization, the London Cigarette Card Company, which devotes boundless effort to the definition and listing of the billions of card issues that have been produced since 1888. An outsider will find their enthusiasm, even fanaticism, quite incomprehensible, especially for modern issues like the Primrose Confectionary Company's 'Dad's Army' series, which received detailed aesthetic and psychological analysis from one magazine contributor. In the same issue another member described his discovery of an unlisted aviation card wrapped with a stick of seaside rock, and commented that 'rock offers a pretty well untouched field for the cartophilist if anyone is sufficiently interested to undertake the research work'. Fortunately appreciation of the Late Victorian and Edwardian issues is more easily shared. The military and theatrical sets issued by the tobacconists James

Taddy and Company appeal instantly to all Victoriana devotees, who delight in the extravagant typography of the slogans and signs on the reverse as well as enjoying the period charm of the portraits in excellent collotype. However, it still needs a specialist to explain the price of well over £200 paid nowadays for the 'Life of Edward VIII' series.

Collectors of the fine arts tend to dismiss cigarette-card collecting as a totally different type of activity from their own intellectual and aesthetic pursuit, yet the cartophilist has much to teach all but the truest aesthetes. For in their fashionable flirtations with collecting, far too many people lack even the most basic understanding of the intrinsic qualities of their hap-hazardly chosen themes. Indeed, the cartophilist epitomizes one of the ideals in collecting, since neither fashion nor profit influences an enthusiasm that stems directly from unpretentious and unstinting regard for the subject.

8 What to buy in the markets

It is exceedingly difficult to offer useful general advice about the things that may be successfully collected on the antique street markets of London, and the subjects listed below have been chosen not because they appeal particu-larly to the author, but in the hope that their variety may lead at least some readers into the pleasures of collecting.

It is only fair to warn aspiring collectors that the general interest in 'antiques' already rides so high that the best and rarest examples in virtually *all* fields will command prices in the hundreds of pounds, however low the average price of the objects collected. The example of cigarette cards has already been quoted, and Edwardian clockwork cars fetched between £400 and £500 at Sotheby's Belgravia in 1973. Even if a collector's field starts by being economical, prices march steadily upwards and sometimes take off completely – witness the sums now paid for Stevengraphs, Fairings, Goss miniatures and pot-lids, all of which were industrial products of the last half of the 19th century, originally sold in their hundreds of thousands for a few pennies each. Certain fields like Studio Pottery and Romantic bronzes which are relatively neglected still demand outlays of up to £150 an object, and if collectors cannot afford to spend such large sums in the first place, there is no consolation in being told that these rare hand-made objects will soon be worth a great deal more.

But, as I suggested earlier in the chapter, a collector's imagination and enthusiasm will quickly open up new possibilities.

In the list which follows I have referred the reader wherever possible to accessible bibliographical sources, the majority being currently obtainable through bookshops, though in many instances detailed information can only be found by research of the original sources in the museums and libraries.

Listed alphabetically, the recommendations may seem oddly assorted, as some subjects like Arts and Crafts furniture are of considerable historical importance, whereas others, like badges, have minimal artistic value in the accepted sense. But all the subjects chosen do appear in the markets, and specialist aspects of each of them are still obtainable without substantial outlay.

Prices are indicated, since the potential collector's degree of interest must necessarily be conditioned by the financial commitment involved; readers must, however, take care to update all price figures as from Spring 1974 when the final proofs of this book were corrected.

Thirty suggestions for collectors

Three examples of Adamesk Pottery. These hand-made and decorated wares are fairly rare, but still extraordinarily cheap when they can be found

Adamesk Pottery Produced only between the years 1904 and 1914, made on Tyneside by Adams and Co. (the firm flourishes still, and now manufactures the most exotic bathroom ceramics in the world). Adameskware is a leadless glazed earthenware in vaguely organic forms, hand thrown, painted and glazed in earthy colours (*left*). Most examples bear the M.J.A. monogram and/or 'Adamesk', impressed. Prices: £10 to £20 each.

The similar Elanware first produced at the same time by Adams and Co. also merits attention, but this pottery is far less rare, being still in production up to the present time. REFERENCE: *Tyneside Pottery* by R. C. Bell (Studio Vista, London 1971).

Art Deco This is one of the cult revivals of the 1970s, life for its followers being somehow incomplete without an Odeon-style juke-box, a Diaghilev ballet costume designed by Bakst and an Eileen Gray black lacquer screen. Those honest enough to admit their ignorance as to what 'Art Deco' actually is can comfort themselves with the knowledge that the experts themselves wrangle over the definition; but the safest line to adopt, so I am told, is that Art Deco first emerged about 1910, appeared fully decked in its camp glory in the Paris Exhibition of 1925, and aged glamorously towards its final demise at the outbreak of World War II.

The most exclusive Art Deco objects fetch gigantic prices but there are many commercial lines that still have all the style, some of the quality and none of the expense. This 'modern style' decanter set has tremendous 'Odeon' decoration

It is still possible to re-create an evocative period atmosphere at a low cost by concentrating on the stylish commercial productions such as Clarice Cliff pottery (the 'Bizarre' set for Wilkinson's was the most distinguished), limousine or submarine teapots, and chunky enamelled glass (*above*). Clothing also has possibilities, with exciting designs in bags, shoes, gloves, etc.; and perhaps one day you'll be lucky enough to find a Sonia Delaunay swimming costume that was actually worn by Noël Coward! All this is possible at well under £50 an item, as opposed to the several hundreds for Argy-Rousseau and Decorchement sculptural glass vases, and several thousand for Rhulmann furniture and the other delights of the wealthy collectors. REFERENCE: *Art Deco* by Bevis Hillier (Studio Vista, London 1968); *The World of Art Deco*. Minneapolis Exhibition Catalogue (Studio Vista, Lon-don 1971); *The Decorative Thirties* by Martin Battersby (Studio Vista, London 1971).

Arts and Crafts Movement Certain artists in the movement are already well known and extensively collected, notably William Morris (1834–96), who was in effect the initiator of the movement in the 1860s, C. R. Ashbee (1863–1942), founder of the Guild of Handicraft in 1888, and Ernest Gimson (1864–1919), leader of the outstanding Gloucestershire craftsmen early this century. But there are many less famous craftsmen whose work sells comparatively cheaply, including many amateurs who were encouraged by dedicated instruction at the newly founded Evening Schools and through the Home Arts and Industries Association (interested collectors need only look through contemporary copies of *The*

Studio for evidence of the quality of amateur work).

The craft movement has many facets, but the following three points of emphasis are suggested to collectors. *Furniture*: The work of important craftsmen often lies unrecognized in the rooms of non-specialist dealers, and collectors should look out for craft qualities in the hand cabinet-work (no use of screws or nails, construction in solid hardwoods, art-metalwork in hinges and mounts, clarity of design, etc.). The more commercial furniture sold in the first decade of this century at shops like Heals and Liberty's was often extremely stylish and should also be considered as part of the movement (*below left*). *Jewellery*: Arts and Crafts jewellery is marvellously varied in its techniques, having been designed and made by artists from different disciplines, including people like the sculptor George Frampton, the enameller Alfred Fisher and

the silversmith Omar Ramsden. Arts and Crafts jewellery offers grateful escape from the encrusted monumentality of the High Victorian, while avoiding the stylistic uniformity of Art Nouveau which was the Continental rage at the time. As everything was individually designed and made, examples are difficult to find but well worth looking for. *Metalwork* (*opposite*): This involves many of the same artists who worked in jewellery, but skills were also fostered in industrial areas like Birmingham where the City Council financed the Vittoria Street School from 1890 and Arthur Dixon founded his own Guild of Handicraft in 1895. In addition there were many independent commercial ventures like that of W. A. S. Benson and Co., which operated successfully until the founder's death in 1920, their hand-wrought copperwares being outstanding.

The prices for some items have already

Only a limited amount of English furniture of the 1900s was positively Art Nouveau in style, but Liberty's products are well worth collecting

This chair was made completely by hand in Kendal by Arthur Simpson in about 1905, and was recently bought by a collector for only £10

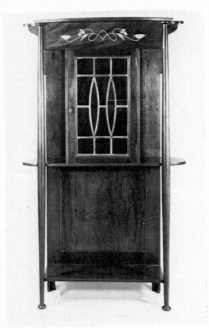

risen to dizzy heights, with Gimson cabinets selling at several thousand pounds, but collectors will find excellently made pieces with purity of design costing far less than good modern products. REFERENCE: *Victorian and Edwardian Decorative Arts*. Exhibition Catalogue, Victoria and Albert Museum (London 1952); *The Schools of Design* by Quentin Bell (Routledge and Kegan Paul, London 1963); *The Arts and Crafts Movement* by Gillian Naylor (Studio Vista, London 1971); *The Arts and Crafts Movement*. Exhibition Catalogue. Fine Art Society (London, Autumn 1973).

Ashtead Pottery Most of these sculptural pottery figures (*p. 78*) are first cousins to the cherubic children in Mabel Lucy Atwell's illustrations and are therefore anathema to many collectors while being irresistible to others. Ashtead Pottery was produced between the years 1926 and 1935, the factory having been set up to teach first world war veterans the potter's craft. Little is heard about Ashtead these days, but it was popular with contemporaries, Harry Trethowan writing in the *Studio Yearbook* of 1929 that 'the work of the Ashtead Pottery is one of the most remarkable developments of Industrial Art', and that 'no bad shapes come out of Ashtead'. A number of significant sculptors were engaged to design the models, including Phoebe and Harold Stabler, Percy Metcalfe and Allan G. Wyon. The sculptors' names are usually moulded in raised letters at the base of the figures, which are of creamy glazed pottery partly painted in dashing thirties colours like tangerine or shark-blue. Most figures also bear the Ashtead printed mark and model number.

Prices can be anything from £5 to £30, the higher sums being paid for models with Art Deco appeal.

Badges A limitless field, encompassing the host of enamel badges of this century produced for members of societies and Trade Unions, for commemorations or awards, or just for decoration and identification.

Many English craftsmen of early this century are still neglected, and quality pieces like this beaten copper rose bowl by John Paul Cooper can be found on market stalls

Enamel badges

Collecting is largely confined to the hippie cult at the present time, but one can confidently predict that the 'Butlin's Second Week' badge, bought last week for the unusually stiff price of 60p, will come under the Sotheby hammer within a decade! Badges have all the properties that excite

Tobacco tins are another amusing field attracting the collector's eye, and some stalls already specialize entirely in tins of various sorts

collectors in other fields: many if not actually dated are at least datable by the event they commemorate, many are marked ('Thomas Fattorini of Birmingham' is an early mark as they later became 'Fattorini and Sons'; but the Birmingham Badge Co. is considered the Wedgwood of badge-makers), and others, like Trade Union badges, have an added historical cachet. Cheshire Street (*see p. 140*) is, the most fertile source of supply.

Average price 10p to 30p, but some are over £1.

Bentwood furniture Despite publicity in the week-end colour supplements there is still very little difference in price between a bentwood chair of early this century and an original of the 1850s, whereas the earlier work has more attractive colouring in the wood, far greater purity in design, and technical superiority in the bending of slimmer pieces of wood. Early bentwood also has a pioneering feel to it, for its factory production by Michel Thonet (1796–1871)

in the 1840s is readily acknowledged as a spiritual precursor of the achievements in modern design at the Bauhaus in the 1920s. Thonet actually founded his own firm in Vienna in 1849, and his designs still seem just as integral to the Viennese scene as they were in the mid-19th century with his commissions for the Palais Lichtenstein and Café Daum.

Distinguished early chairs can be bought for £30 to £40 each, and tables from £60 to £80. REFERENCE: *Bentwood Furniture.* Exhibition Catalogue. Bethnal Green Museum (London 1968); *Il Caso Thonet* by Georgio Santoro (Rome 1966).

Biscuit, tobacco and other tins Nothing was beyond the ingenuity of Edwardian biscuit manufacturers, who sold their products in tins formed as children's toys, clock garnitures, the Taj Mahal, and any other incongruous shape that came to mind. Tobacconists were equally imaginative, with tins painted to simulate malachite or formed as capstans to contain, respective-

Almost every English ceramic manufacturer in the 19th century produced blue and white transfer ware, which gives collectors an exciting selection to choose from

ly, their Russian and Naval tobaccos. Providing care is taken over condition, an adventurous collection can make enchanting decoration.

The most desirable tin I have ever spotted was only £12, and the majority are far less expensive.

Blue and White Transfer Ware (*above*): There is always satisfaction in the visual uniformity of a tightly defined collection, and a provincial Welsh dresser stacked with a piecemeal blue and white service formed from various sources can look stunning. Transfer printing of this kind was invented in the 1780s and developed to confident complexity in the early 19th century. The wares were made largely for export and cover all items from soup-tureens to napkin-rings, in all styles from Gothic to Grecian. They were made by almost every English factory.

Price depends on rarity of the item and the complexity of decoration, but new collectors need spend no more than £8 to

£15 on each object. REFERENCE: *Blue and White Transfer Ware 1780–1840* by A. W. Coysh (David and Charles, Newton Abbot 1970); *Blue and White Earthenware 1800–1850* by A. W. Coysh (David and Charles, Newton Abbot 1973).

Bois Durci medallions Bois Durci lays claim to be the father of modern plastics, the commercial process having been patented in France and England in 1855. The basic ingredients were rosewood sawdust and albumen (bull's blood was often used), and this was poured into pressurized moulds to make numerous domestic objects including knife handles, chessmen, jewellery and furniture mounts. However the most collectable product was a remarkable series of portrait medallions of both contemporary and historical characters (*p. 96*). The image on these four and a half inch diameter roundels is perfectly crisp and smooth, and the full black colour gives them a bronze-like quality. Original examples are inscribed 'Bois Durci' on the reverse, and

A whole series of Bois Durci portrait medallions was issued. They sell from between £3 and £6 each and form a marvellous collecting entity

are also stamped below the portrait with a small winged emblem. Amazingly the interest in this most collectable series is minimal and each one need cost no more than £3 to £6. REFERENCE: *Tunbridge and Scottish Souvenir Woodware* (with chapters on Bois Durci and Pyrography) by E. H. and E. R. Pinto (G. Bell and Sons, London 1970).

Bottles The ideal collecting hobby for those with an incurable fascination with pure junk, because the greatest bottle finds are made literally in rubbish dumps. Indeed, rival collectors are continuously improving methods of locating municipal dumps that have been disguised for years beneath allotments and farm fields.

Early wine bottles provide an obvious appeal, but 19th-century soft-drink and medicine bottles also have pleasing shapes and colours. Bottle-collecting clubs have already been formed, and their members can easily be identified on Sunday afternoons standing knee-deep in water peering through glass-bottomed buckets at Thames-side sludge as it is turned over by their 'digging partners'.

Bottles can be purchased for very small sums, but collectors will doubtless prefer to find their own rather than pay for them. REFERENCE: *Bottle Collecting* by Edward Fletcher (Blandford Press, London 1972).

Bronzes Few undiscovered areas in the fine arts still exist, but English 19th-century Romantic bronzes is one of these. Almost any bronze will cost at least £30, so that the outlay for a collection could be considerable, but the expense would be justified as the high-ranking qualities of the New Sculpture especially (produced in England from about 1870 to 1915) will soon receive worldwide recognition. One of the delights of these bronzes is the life and light given to surface details through the sculptors' revival of the sensitive 'lost-wax' method of casting bronzes; the sculptors were also encouraged during this period to be highly personal in their choice of subject-matter

and this naturally lead to imaginative variations of form.

Most of these bronze statuettes were hand cast in limited editions, and practically all are signed; names to watch out for include Alfred Gilbert, Goscombe John, George Frampton, R.F. Wells, Charles Sykes, Onslow Ford, Alfred Drury and W. Reynolds Stevens.

Prices vary widely, but almost any good example is worth buying at present-day average prices. REFERENCE: *British Sculpture 1850 to 1915*. Exhibition Catalogue (Fine Art Society, London 1968); *Nineteenth Century Romantic Bronzes* by Jeremy Cooper (David and Charles, Newton Abbot 1974).

Charles Vyse pottery figures Charles Vyse was one of the interesting transitional artists connecting turn-of-the-century Studio Pottery with modern craft pottery. He was trained in Staffordshire from 1896, but set up his own pottery in Cheyne Row, Chelsea, in 1919, where he worked throughout his life except for a short absence during the second world war. Charles modelled all the groups and his wife Nell was responsible for the colouring, glazing and firing. Their most stylish work was in the allegorical figures and groups influenced in style by Continental Art Deco

W. Reynolds Stevens designed and made furniture, silver, sculpture and other objects, and this relief bronze frame, dated 1896, is typical of his adventurous taste

It is quite conceivable that this unsigned bronze bust by Onslow Ford could turn up on a market stall at under £100, although its full value is nearer £1,000

In the early 1970s Charles Vyse's work could still be bought for £10 to £20. Collectors can expect similar rises in value of other things that are still cheap. The dog vendors (top left) still gather on Club Row (see page 75)

(left), but the realistic figures are also most appealing (above). Early models were occasionally produced in relatively large numbers, but later figures were issued in editions of twenty or less.

Prices vary considerably and are likely to increase noticeably over the next few years but anything between £80 and £150 is still reasonable for a Vyse figure.

Children's books Second-hand bookshop browsing is one of the few bad habits that need never be broken; however many apparently wasted hours it may consume, the comforts and pleasures of bookshops are too precious to be denied. While early children's books are expensively shelved by the antiquarian booksellers, there are still exciting prospects for less wealthy collectors in the period 1850 to 1930. This period begins with the developments in wood-engraving of master printers like Dalziel, and incorporates some romantic illustration by the Pre-Raphaelite painters; but the real breakthrough in children's books naturally came with advances in colour printing. In the last three decades of the 19th century English book illustration blossomed into

W. Heath Robinson was a marvellous illustrator of children's books, and The Water Babies, *from which these are taken, could be purchased on the markets for £10 to £15 in first edition, and far less in a subsequent printing*

the lyrical artistry of Walter Crane, Randolph Caldecott, Kate Greenaway and many others including James and Richard Doyle, whose work for the publisher Edmund Evans merits the closest attention (Richard Doyle's *In Fairyland* of 1870 reveals an amazing delicacy of touch coupled with a way-out imagination).

From early in this century, Arthur Rackham is well known though perhaps over-rated (except in his outstanding *Kensington Gardens* and *Midsummer Night's Dream*); W. Heath Robinson (*above*) was far more varied in style and, at £10 to £15 each, his books are two-thirds the price of Rackham. The new collector may prefer to concentrate on even later illustrators, like Hugh Thomson, who, at £5 or £8 for the smaller uncoloured volumes, are excellent value. But then there are so many appealing angles to 19th-century children's book collecting, which range from the evocative Henty adventure books to the esoteric products

of the private presses run by Charles Ricketts, Cobden Sanderson and the rest. REFERENCE: *The Victorian Illustrated Book* by Percy Muir (Batsford, London 1971). *Victorian Book Design* by Ruari Maclean (re-printed London 1972); *The Art Nouveau Book in Britain* by John Russell Taylor (Methuen, London 1966).

Cigarette cards The collecting of Late Victorian and Edwardian cigarette cards should not be summarily dismissed as a childhood hangover. The cards issued by the tobacconists James Taddy and Company, fondly known as 'Taddy's', have the greatest period charm, especially their set of 125 'V.C. Heroes', giving names, regiments and the dates of the 'acts of bravery' (six soldiers appear with false credentials, there being no record of their awards). Another favourite is Ogden's 'Actresses and Beauties' issued between 1895 and 1899 in four separate sets of fifty. They were among the last cards to be printed by the Wood-burytype photographic process, and Miss Esmond White winking over the top of her fan is typical of their considerable charms.

Would-be cartophilists should subscribe to the monthly magazine *Cigarette Card News*, founded in 1933 by Colonel Charles Bagnall, and at present edited with considerable panache by his daughter, Dorothy Bagnall, whose periodic auctions at Caxton Hall are not to be missed. Prices of early sets average at £6, but the 'Life of Edward VIII' series fetches over £200. REFERENCE: *Collecting Cigarette Cards* by Dorothy Bagnall (London Cigarette Card Company, 1973); *British Cigarette Card Issues 1888–1940* (reprinting, LCCC).

David d'Angers medallions European markets are obviously better than the London stalls for these bronze medallions by the French sculptor P.J. David (1788–1856), called David d'Angers, but there are still many to be found in England. Although basically Neoclassical in his style and one of the leading academic sculptors of his time, David had the inherently

The painter Théodore Géricault by David d'Angers, who made over five hundred such portraits

Romantic idea of producing privately a remarkable series of portrait medallions of over five hundred famous contemporaries from all over Europe and America. These small bronze reliefs are almost completely uncollected, despite certainly being the first, and arguably, among the best Romantic portrait sculpture. All examples are signed either 'P.J. David', 'David d'Angers', or just 'David', and the large majority are inscribed with the sitter's name.

Examples can still be secured for as little as £20, though £40–£60 is their average price.

Della Robbia Pottery This hand-thrown and painted pottery has the attraction to collectors of only having been produced during twelve years, from 1884 to 1896, although it was of a quality to receive Royal patronage during this short time. The Pottery was founded by Harold Rathbone, who engaged the help of two eminent sculptors, Conrad Dressler (1856–1940) and Robert Anning Bell (1863–1933). It specialized in bold forms in faience-pottery, and the decorations were often inspired by Renaissance motifs, although some of their most successful work relied more on naturalistic details. They also produced some splendid tiles designed for them exclusively by the Pre-Raphaelite painter Edward Burne-Jones. An average vase will cost about £20 these days, but prices are rising rapidly and a highly decorative wall plaque recently secured £65 at auction.

Eggs and egg cups A cabinetful of egg-cups is much more striking than the collections of glass scent bottles that are so popular. Collectors must accept the sad fact that they have little chance of finding, or of affording, were it found, the first recorded egg-cup, of which Lady Hervey wrote in 1690: 'Dear Cosen donn gave me a silver ege thing worth ten ginnes [*sic*]'; but both egg-cups and egg-frames became very popular during the late 18th century, in porcelain as well as in silver. However, rarity and price may lead collectors to specialize in Victorian examples, which come in all media and the most un-egglike shapes. One can always start a complementary collection of eggs themselves, in which the choice ranges from Russian eggs in jewelled hardstone to hand-painted Moldavian batik eggs. It all gives one's house-guests something to talk about at breakfast. REFERENCE: *An Egg at Easter* by Venetia Newell (Routledge and Kegan Paul, London 1973).

Encaustic tiles Collectors will have even better luck with these on building demolition sites than in the markets, as practically every Victorian house had at least one floor in encaustic tiles, following the example of Queen Victoria at Osborne in 1844 and of President Arthur at the United States Capitol in 1855. Encaustic tiles were fired in inch-thick terracotta with coloured slip clays inlaid in stylized patterns, which made them particularly hard-wearing. Samuel Wright was granted an English patent for the encaustic process in 1830 and Herbert Minton immediately joined him in the venture. This particular patent expired in 1844, by which time Minton, with large expenditures of money and enthusiasm, had developed superb techniques that were never quite rivalled by later practitioners like Godwin and Maw.

Collectors will have to defend their hobby against ridicule by supporters of the later hand-painted 'art tiles', but encaustic tiles, being a basic design entity, delightfully reflect the whole spectrum of High Victorian taste; and anyway, at only £1 or £2 each they have a distinct economic advantage over the more expensive art tiles.

Many encaustic tiles are marked with the name of the makers and the date of registration of the design; and many famous designers, ranging from A. W. N. Pugin, Gothic decorator of the Houses of Parliament, to Christopher Dresser, the eminent botanist, designed for the tile manufacturers. REFERENCE: *Victorian Ceramic Tiles* by Julian Barnard (Studio Vista, London 1972).

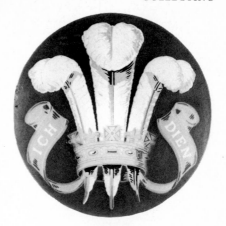

These two large encaustic tiles of heraldic design are outstanding examples and relatively costly, but most sell at £1 to £2 each and are great fun to collect.

Goss first world war miniatures Goss is worth a mention if only to provide an excuse to draw your attention to the most enchanting collector's handbook in print, *Goss China* by J. Galpin. Mr Galpin's little book testifies to the extraordinary expertise a private collector can acquire, with dedication; though many will deny that Goss is worthy of so much reverence.

W. H. Goss (died 1906) began his production of standard terracotta and porcelain wares in 1858, and did not turn to his miniature heraldic porcelain until the

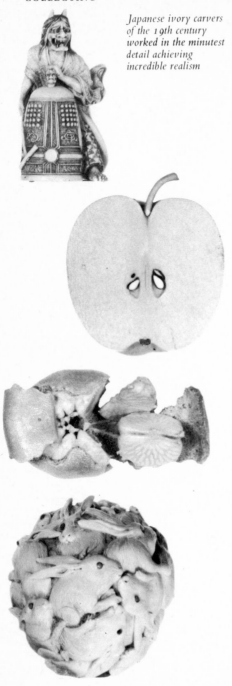

Japanese ivory carvers of the 19th century worked in the minutest detail achieving incredible realism

1880s. Despite the immense success of this line, the factory he had founded was in financial difficulties by 1914; the situation was saved by the introduction of a series of almost two hundred different first world war miniatures. A splendid parade of cartoon-like mini-tanks, mortars and battleships appeared, along with the star of any collection, the contact mine, celebrated by a private issue in 1919 for the already formed League of Goss Collectors.

In a recent sale, an earlier miniature, *The Old Smithy, Gullane*, secured an astounding £260, while an incendiary bomb, a tank and two other wartime pieces in one lot fetched the more likely sum of £18. So cash in your Goss cottages while the going is good and switch interests to the neglected first world war series! REFERENCE: *Goss China* by J. Galpin (published privately in 1972).

Japanese ivory okimonos The cool touch of a half-peeled satsuma realistically carved and coloured in ivory momentarily confuses perception (*left*). Strictly speaking, an 'okimono' is a free-standing figurative group in ivory, but realistic carvings of fruit, intricately carved imaginative compositions and other creations are generally included under this general heading. These ivories have astonishing technical qualities; and besides, the collector will soon find himself exploring the world of Eastern legend to explain the strange antics of the 'onis', 'sennin' and other creatures who inhabit the imagination of Japanese artists. Many have a symbolic theme similar to the Noh plays; others just record the onis' mischievous hauntings and tricks. The most absorbing okimonos illustrate classical legends, like the 10th-century tale of Kiyohime, an innkeeper's daughter who fell in love with a philandering monk; on discovering her unexpected devotion, the monk hid from her under a bell. In the form of a dragon (*top left*) she alighted on the bell and beat it with her tail until the white heat consumed them both.

The prices of earlier Japanese carvings

are already astronomically high, but a good 19th-century collection is still possible at an average price of £40 to £70 per item, although the finest pieces will necessarily cost £150 or more. REFERENCE: *Pointers and Clues for the Subjects of Chinese and Japanese Art* by W.H. Edwards (Sampson, Low, Marston, London 1934); *Legend in Japanese Art* by H.L. Joly (Kegan Paul Trench, Trubner and Co., London, reprinted 1973).

Jewellery Virtually every other stall in Bermondsey and Portobello has at least some jewellery, so the collector has a tremendous choice of sources. It is impossible to tackle the subject seriously without specialization, and some of the alternatives include: *Jet* The production of jet jewellery was almost an industry at Whitby in Yorkshire, in the 19th century, with fifty workshops in 1850 and over two hundred in 1873, all turning out fashionable mourning-wear. But collectors must take care not to mistake jet, which is cut from cannel-coal, for French black glass jewellery of the same period. *Cut and polished steel* Quite a lot of steel jewellery was already being produced at Woodstock in Oxfordshire in the mid-18th century. Indeed the best examples will all be pre-Victorian, for by 1840 the industry was in decline. As its popularity coincided with a period of elaborate male fashion, cut-steel decoration for men – buckles, chatelaines and buttons – is often as exotic as the bangles and baubles of female attire. *Berlin Iron* Like cut-steel jewellery 'Berlin Iron' always seems quintessentially Victorian, although its heyday was also in fact earlier, during Empire/Regency times. The first factory for its production was founded in Berlin in 1804, and it was still being successfully shown at the international exhibitions of the mid-century. Its scarcity would suggest that production remained limited, so that its quality was not jeopardized by the later commercialism of industrial manufacture. Much Berlin Iron jewellery has the added interest of bearing makers' marks.

Jet jewellery is still comparatively cheap, attractive examples costing no more than £10, but both Berlin Iron and cut and polished steel have become so scarce that elaborate early pieces sell for well over £100. REFERENCE: *Victorian Jewellery* by Margaret Fowler (Cassell, London 1967); *Cut-Steel and Berlin Iron Jewellery* by Anne Clifford (Adams and Dart, London 1971).

Linthorpe Pottery The Linthorpe Pottery in Yorkshire was the brainchild of perhaps the most revolutionary design-theorist of the 19th century, Christopher Dresser, a botanist who, inspired by Japanese aesthetics, abstracted pure linear forms from his study of plants. He was backed in 1879 by a moneyed landowner named John Harrison from Middlesbrough in Yorkshire, and the Linthorpe Pottery was constructed on the site of the latter's Sun Brick Works. The Pottery actually ceased production in 1889, and the earliest years were the most successful (collectors should look for the impressed monograms H.T., standing for the first manager Henry Tooth, and A.F., for Arthur Fuller, their most distinguished potter). Dresser experimented in a combination of organic and classical shapes, as well as producing those thick, equatorial glazes (*p. 104*) that distinguish the ceramics at Linthorpe and at her sister potteries, Bretby and Ault.

There is little reason to spend more than £50 on the very best Linthorpe piece, and individual purchases will average nearer £20 to £30. REFERENCE: *Linthorpe Pottery*. Teeside Museum and Art Gallery, 1970; *Christopher Dresser*. Exhibition Catalogue. Fine Art Society, with Richard Dennis and John Jesse (London 1972).

Photographs Only a few years ago early photographs could be bought by the folder for a handful of old pennies, and many people who had then been buying photographs purely for their visual or topographical qualities without any knowledge of the photographers, now find themselves with choice Camerons or Hill/Adamsons

Three examples of Linthorpe Pottery which was founded in 1879 by Christopher Dresser, one of the most important designers of the 19th century

worth £400 to £600 each. But the subject is still young, and many more fascinating photographers are still unknown, so there is plenty of scope. Some collectors will be attracted to photographs of an aesthetic quality similar to painting (e.g. Hill/ Adamson, *opposite top*), others to those of historical or topographical interest (e.g. Thomson and Smith, and others again to the technical specialities (e.g. Eadweard Muybridge, *opposite below*). Modern literature on early photography is so stimulating that no more need be done here than to refer the reader to the available sources, where he will find all the details clearly stated.

As already mentioned, the prices for some photographers is already high, but Muybridge prints, for example, are only £30 to £50 each at the moment, and many attractive early photographs by unknown artists are sold for a mere £1 or £2. REFERENCE: *A Concise History of Photography* by H. and A. Gernsheim (Thames and Hudson, London 1965); *The Begin-*

nings of Photography, 'From Today Painting is Dead.' Exhibition Catalogue. Victoria and Albert Museum (1972); *Early Photographs and Photographers* by Oliver Matthews (Reedminster Publications, London 1973).

Portobello Pottery This was made on the Firth of Forth, not in Notting Hill, although both 'Portobello' foundations commemorate Admiral Vernon's victory in 1739 at Puerto Bello in the Gulf of Mexico. William Jameson erected a brick kiln in the tiny Portobello hamlet east of Edinburgh in 1763, and this grew into the official Portobello Pottery in 1786, when it was leased to the Scott brothers (early wares bear their name and often the impressed monogram P.B.). In 1808 the ownership of the pottery passed to Thomas Yoole and his son-in-law Thomas Rathbone, and it operated with considerable success until the recession of 1837–38 led directly to its closure in 1850. It had produced some charming clay figures and plaques, simply enamelled in the

Though this famous photograph of the Newhaven Fishermen sells at auction for between £400 and £600, there are many unknown photographers whose work sells for a few pounds only and makes exciting collecting

In the 1870s Eadweard Muybridge published these important studies of human motion; his first aim was to help the accuracy of artistic representation, but the possibility of developing such techniques to make moving pictures was quickly acknowledged to have far wider significance

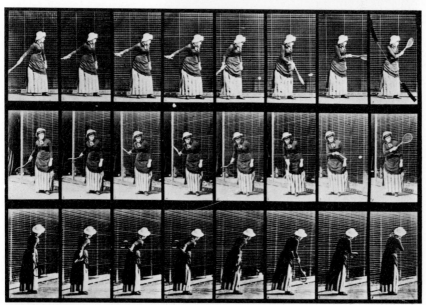

Staffordshire tradition; some of the ware such as the Florentine lions was made in large numbers for export, but most examples of Portobello Pottery are rare, and it appeals to those who like to concentrate on lesser known factories. Individual items need cost no more than £15 to £30 each.

Postcards 'Sent with affection to swell your collection' was a favourite inscription on Edwardian cards, which were fashionably collected by contemporaries. The first picture postcard was printed in October 1870, though it carried nothing more adventurous than the Royal Coat of Arms, and imaginative design was inevitably curtailed until the divided back was invented in about 1904, allowing the whole of one side to be used for illustration. Recently market stallholders have begun to present postcards for sale in sorted categories and sets to satisfy collectors, whose specialities range from Middle Eastern topographical cards, through theatrical erotica to broad seaside humour. Some of the best cards include Raphael Kirchner's artistic pin-ups to titillate the troops (for example 'A Duck's Egg', showing nothing but the long stockinged legs of a chorus girl emerging from inside a broken egg); other favourites are James Bamforth's or Donald McGill's cheerful holiday smut, and the louche three-dimensional cards of first world war heroes.

A Mucha postcard can cost as much as £5, and a set of 'The Dreyfus Affair' perhaps £12, but a single card is not normally more than 20p to 50p.

Printwork embroidery These embroidered pictures are among the most exquisite examples of the needlewoman's craft, in which black silks are normally used on a white silk ground to imitate engraving. Rare examples employ silks graded in shade from black through grey to cream (*right*), and the rarest of all use human hair instead of silk. There are still many 18th-century examples about, but good condition and lack of fading are important.

Printwork embroidery sells for about £10 to £30. REFERENCE: *The Saturday Book 1973* (an article by Susan Lasdun).

Records In 1891 Emile Berliner produced the first disc record, and for the seventy-eight record buff life on earth might as well not have existed before this date.

These three postcards are selected from a remarkable collection of over 150 cards which were sent by one English soldier during the first world war to his fiancée who was a lady's maid at Eton College in Windsor. Such cards sell at 20p to 40p each on the markets

A fine example of printwork embroidery from the early 19th century. Silks were normally used, but rarer examples are executed in human hair to imitate engraving

The record-collecting ambience is steeped in nostalgia, and echoes with the rival claims of the classic (and most expensive) early operatic recordings, the dance bands of the twenties, and the music-hall stars of the 1900s. Condition and quality of sound are crucial to most collectors, but enthusiasts would pay £20 for a Caruso Zonophone Blue record even in two pieces.

The novice collector will soon find his conversation peppered with gossip about Emma Albani or Amadeo Bassi, and a pile of Fonotopia label records will gradually grow higher and higher beside an early 'graphophone'. The history and romance of the period adds to the enjoyment of collecting, and a true devotee will delight just as much in a conversation with an old lady who actually performed in those early, hazardous days of sound recording, as in possessing one of the first double-sided records of 1905.

Search for rarities can take the enthusiast anywhere, but a viable collection can still be amassed with an average outlay of £1 or £2 per record, despite the prices of up to £500 paid for an original Berliner. REFERENCE: *Historical Records 1898–1908/9* by R. Bauer (Sidgwick and Jackson, London 1970); *Vertical Cut Cylinders and Discs*. A catalogue of all Hill and Dale recordings of serious worth issued between 1897 and 1932, by Girard and Barnes (British Institute of Recorded Sound, 1971).

Sheet music covers Infatuation with the music-hall is helpful but not essential to the enjoyment of this grand, popular art. The decoration of sheet music became practical with the development in the late 1830s of

Such a hand-driven Berliner gramophone of the early 1890s could cost up to £1,000. On the markets slightly later talking machines still sell for considerably less than they are securing in specialist auction sales, and there would certainly be a chance of finding similar rarities at nominal sums

chromolithography (colour printing from chalk-drawn stone blocks), and the first song-writer to take advantage of this new process was Julien, who published his first popular song in 1844. Julien died from acute depression in 1856, after Covent Garden Opera House burned down with all his scores inside, and he therefore did not benefit from the elaboration of the illustrator's art in the 1860s by artists such as Alfred Concanen (1835–86).

A Concanen music cover even in bad condition is likely to cost at least £3, and £50 or so may be asked for the best. But the music-hall boom of 1860–70 gave work to hundreds of lesser artists, some of whom, notably Maguire the Younger and Hamentor, are underpriced by comparison at less than £1 a cover. REFERENCE: *Victorian Sheet Music Covers* by R. Pearsall

(David and Charles, Newton Abbot 1972); *Victorian Sheet Music Covers* by D. and S. Spellman (Adams and Mackay, London 1969).

Talking machines The unconverted should begin with a visit to Fagin's Phonograph Emporium at 46 Hornsey Road, London N.7, to see the amazing assortment of talking machines with their bizarre varieties of horns. Edison's tinfoil phonograph in 1877 was the first, although one of the most coveted machines is the comparatively late Edison Opera Phonograph of 1912. Even a pocket phonograph was produced, an extraordinary machine presumably intended to provide entertainment at Edwardian picnics.

Prices vary according to where collectors buy, and the age and condition of the instrument. An early hand-driven Berliner gramophone has recently secured £1,000 at auction, and the prices of ordinary Edison Gem phonographs are mounting daily, but an exciting representative collection of early gramophones and phonographs need average no more than £60 an item, especially if the collector has the knowledge to repair damaged machines. REFERENCE: *Talking Machines* by V.K. Chew (Science Museum Publications, London 1967).

Victorian crafts This is a huge field, incorporating all the now-forgotten crafts practised by sheltered Victorian ladies, and collectors can be selective or catholic in their tastes. The most ingenious techniques were employed to produce more or less artistic creations out of improbable materials, such as dried seaweed, partridge feathers, rolled paper and human hair. Some of these unlikely pieces possess undeniable aesthetic qualities: rolled paper tea-caddies and some cork pictures come to mind. Other artifacts such as shell sculpture and tinsel pictures can claim no more than period charm.

Prices range from £1 upwards. REFERENCE: *Regency and Victorian Crafts* by Jane Toller (Ward Lock, London 1969).

Many Victorian crafts fail to achieve such genuine artistic quality as this cork picture of a palace beside a lake; but the collection of all Victorian crafts provides considerable enjoyment

9 How to buy in the markets

Some fortunate people simply have a nose for bargains, and nothing much can be done about it if you have not. All the same, even for these lucky collectors, the only way to buy consistently well on the markets is to back up a sound knowledge of current taste and values with sheer hard work. The hard work consists in tramping up to six or seven miles before breakfast every Friday morning, up and down the lines of stalls at Bermondsey, catching the stallholders just as they unpack the week's findings; and then following this up on Saturday with perhaps three or four hours of combing the Portobello. This may sound excessive, but people discipline themselves to such a routine, and until one does so oneself there is no justification for begrudging them their discoveries.

The first lesson to learn is that interesting items can turn up on *any* stall in the market; indeed, as every successful salesman knows, deals can be clinched in the most unlikely places, and collectors should never dismiss a stall merely because it had been barren on previous occasions. The vast majority of stallholders have a thoroughly catholic taste, buying and selling as much what they like as what they know about; this means that some items which are decorative but undistinguished may be overpriced, but conversely plenty of others with which the sellers are not fully familiar may be marked down, and this is how real discoveries can be made by the specialist collector. Indeed the specialist will often do better to ignore the stalls concentrating on his field, and instead to ferret about among the odds and ends in remote corners and dark alleys.

The actual purchasing of goods on the markets is greatly helped by cash payment; indeed advantage in battle is assured by the deft deployment of a top pocketful of bank-notes. Some regulars revel in the striking of a bargain with the stallholder, and tactics range from putting on the impoverished but keen collector's act, through ridicule, to the subtle game of concealing from the seller the identity of the interesting object by asking questions about almost everything else on the stall, finally slipping under his guard with a casual, 'Oh well, and what's the price of *that* then?'

There is, of course, a completely different code of selling between dealer and dealer, and private buyers used to bluff their way to being allowed 'trade terms'. But the game has been played once too often, so that nowadays 'trade terms' are offered almost automatically and do not always represent a reduction. The present state of the bargaining game was made apparent to a dealer-friend when he stopped at a stall to ask the price of a silver snuff-box, and was told £50; after lengthy exchanges the seller decided that the lowest offer he could possibly accept was £46, and 'that's trade terms'. When the dealer-buyer produced his trade account book, the stallholder was quick to apologize, saying 'Oh well, if you really *are* trade, the price is only £38.' In these circumstances one may actually do better in buying from the older dealers who insist on the full asking price, except for marginal reductions to their regular clients.

This brings us to the crucial question of value. First it should be pointed out, even at the risk of stating the obvious, that no art object has a precise financial value. In effect a painting or clock or any art object is worth exactly what anyone is prepared to pay for it. This rule is made clear every day in the auction rooms, when objects are proved to be worth previously inconceivable sums to at least two people, though the rest of the audience, however expert, would have given perhaps a tenth of the sum bid.

In general the street markets offer goods at fair prices, and there is far less danger of spending an irrecoverable sum at a stall than at a smart West End shop where large overheads automatically fix the prices at a high level. The most important precaution for collectors is to look around to establish the 'going' values in their field, and with this in mind, to buy at the kind of prices that have meaning to their particular collections. In no time the enthusiastic amateur finds that instinct develops into expertise, and then purchases can be made in complete confidence.

In my experience the worst mistakes are made by collectors buying purely for profit in a field with which they are not fully conversant. A brave buy may produce a tidy profit, but equally, pieces that appeared cheap may turn out to have a later mark, or to have been repaired, or to be inferior in some esoteric way. However, the casual user of the markets *must* buy purely on personal taste, and providing the price is not beyond his or her pocket, anything that really appeals is, by definition, 'good value'.

There are no rules of conduct in any of the markets, but simple, unasser-tive friendliness will bring the most success. The majority of stallholders regularly brave the cold and discomfort of the open streets because they enjoy the comradeship and shared interests of an amusing and individualistic crowd of people. They will therefore form relationships with their regular clients with keen pleasure. Personal contact once established will allow dealers to keep their eyes open for the collector's particular interest, though there will be no obligation to buy; and as a genuine collector, the regular will find himself directed all over the market by helpful stallholders who have heard that so-and-so has 'your sort of thing'.

Critics of the markets claim that the good things are overpriced, the better things have already been sold, and the best things are stolen. Even if this were true (which it is not), it would still be worth going, just for the pleasure of being part of so free and lively a scene.

Part Three: Guide to the Markets

10 The Portobello Market

A. Days and times of opening

The Portobello Market is divided into several areas with varying times of opening as indicated below.

The principal antique street market functions on SATURDAY, from 8.30 a.m. to 5.30 p.m.

The antique and bric-a-brac market beneath the Westway motorway flyover functions on FRIDAY and SATURDAY, from 8 a.m. to about 5.30 p.m. (The permitted trading hours of these street markets are longer, but in practice the hours of business are generally as stated above. Bad weather keeps some stallholders away but the majority will be there in all conditions. In winter, however, afternoon trading is curtailed by the shorter hours of daylight.)

The antique arcades and enclosed stalls on the Portobello Road open on SATURDAY from 7.30 a.m. to 5.30 p.m. A few also open on FRIDAY, when business is light.

The large number of antique shops on and around the Portobello Road do a flourishing trade throughout the week, Saturdays included, during normal opening hours.

Visitors on Saturday will find the Portobello full of people throughout the mile of markets, and many street-sellers, musicians and entertainers mingling with the crowds. But this busy road is never too rough or noisy, and stallholders and shopkeepers are invariably courteous and helpful. The Portobello Road is due to be closed officially to through motor traffic, and is already almost impassable for cars.

Keen collectors should try to attend regularly on Saturdays from 7.45 a.m. to

about 9.30 a.m., when the stalls are being set up and a swift exchange occurs of some of the best offerings of the day.

B. Range of items available, and prices

Over the last decade the Portobello Market has grown in such a way that now, either on the Road itself or in the immediate neighbourhood, antiques and second-hand objects of every size, age and description are to be found. Specialists exist for practically every collectable subject, and these specialist stalls and shops are listed according to subject in section E below, and are also marked on the Portobello maps.

The list and maps are intended for those who have only a limited time to spend on the Portobello Market and may wish to concentrate on a few specialists. Collectors who become Saturday regulars will soon realize that objects of specific interest can turn up on any of the several thousand stalls in the market.

Prices vary throughout the Road, some dealers being expensive and others cheap. As a general rule the pieces of lesser quality tend to be rather expensive for what they are, while the good things are not overpriced. Bargains abound for those with luck and/or expertise.

C. Public transport

(see also Portobello Area map, p. 123)

UNDERGROUND: Notting Hill Gate is the most convenient station (Central, Circle and District Lines). From the station (northern exit) there is a three-minute walk along Pembridge Road to the beginning of the Portobello Road, which branches off on the left. The market itself begins about a quarter of a mile down the Road.

Ladbroke Grove (Metropolitan Line) and Westbourne Park stations (also Metropolitan Line) are both within an eight-minute walk of the lower (northern) end of the market, down Lancaster Road.

BUSES: 52 stops within sight of the market, at *Kensington Park Gardens*, and again at *Elgin Crescent*. It runs from Victoria *via* Hyde Park Corner, High Street Kensington, Kensington Church Street and Notting Hill Gate (final destination Mill Hill). 15 stops within sight of the market at *Westbourne Grove* and again at *Elgin Crescent*. It runs from East Ham *via* Strand, Piccadilly Circus, Marble Arch and Paddington Station (final destination Ladbroke Grove). 7 stops within sight of the northern end of the market at *Westbourne Park Road*. From Oxford Circus *via* Marble Arch, Paddington and Ladbroke Grove (final destination Acton). 12, 27, 28, 31, 88 all stop within five minutes' walk of the market at *Notting Hill Gate*. 27 from Teddington *via* Kensington (final destination Highgate). 28 from Wandsworth *via* Kensington (final destination Golders Green Station). 31 from Chelsea *via* Kensington (final destination Camden Town). 12 from Norwood Junction *via* Piccadilly Circus and Marble Arch (final destination Harlesden). 88 from Mitcham *via* Trafalgar Square and Oxford Circus (final destination Acton Green).

D. Food and drink, local entertainment

The sources of food and drink on the Portobello fall broadly into the four categories below (references in brackets are locations on the Portobello detail maps, pages 124–9).

COFFEE AND SNACKS
Dolphin Antiques. 157 Portobello Rd. (C4) *Excellent service at tables among the upstairs stalls. Home-made sandwiches, cakes, etc.*

Weaver Arcade. 73 Portobello Rd. (E11) *A secluded little snack bar offering salads, etc. in cheerful surroundings.*

Casa Maria. 125 Portobello Rd. (D6) *Good for breakfast and hot snacks.*

Red Lion. 169 Portobello Rd. (B3) *Coffee and sandwiches on the third floor.*

Hovis Bakery. 131 Portobello Rd. (D5) *Take-away sandwiches and rolls.* *Also ice-cream and Coca-Cola from stall outside.*

Hot-dog stall. Outside Carpenters, 162 Portobello Rd.

Snack Bar. Corner Portobello Antique Supermarket. 282 Westbourne Grove. (C6) *On the second floor with open-air seating overlooking the market.*

Bona's Café. 160 Portobello Rd. *Located at beginning of fruit market. Standard café food.*

PUBS
Henekey's The Earl of Lonsdale. Corner of Portobello Rd–Westbourne Grove. (E7) *Traditional pub snacks. Mulled wine in winter, beer garden open in summer.*

Finch's Duke of Wellington. 179 Portobello Rd. (D2) *Hippie rallying-point. Impromptu lunchtime concerts.*

Finch's Wine Cellar. 120 Kensington Park Rd. (C8)

The Portobello Star. 171 Portobello Rd. (D2)

The Princess Alexandra. 95 Portobello Rd. (E9)

DELICATESSEN AND FOOD SHOPS
Jennings. 11 Elgin Crescent. *Continental delicatessen run by the friendly Cheeseman family. Opens Sunday mornings too.*

Hawkins. 197 Portobello Rd. *Sells hot sausage rolls as well as continental meats, sausages, etc.*

Ceres Bakery and Natural Food Shop. 269 Portobello Rd. *Macrobiotic foods (and literature).*

The Jamaican Pattie Company. 261 Portobello Rd. *The real thing.*

RESTAURANTS
The immediate neighbourhood has com-

paratively few restaurants, but the following are close to the market:

L'Artiste Assoiffé (727 4714), 306 Westbourne Grove (C8) *and* Leith's (229 4481), 92 Kensington Park Rd. *Both have fine reputations, the latter being particularly expensive.*

Duveen. 29 Kensington Park Rd. (A1) *Excellent French cooking at low prices. Individual atmosphere.*

The Courtyard. Pembridge Rd, opposite the beginning of Portobello Rd. *Steaks their speciality. Reasonable prices.*

Corndolly Wholefood Vegetarian Restaurant. 307 Westbourne Park Rd, just by Portobello Rd.

Going westwards towards Holland Park and Shepherd's Bush the gourmet has a wide choice of fine restaurants within walking distance, the most tempting of which are:

Julie's (229 8331), 135 Portland Road.

La Pomme d'Amour (229 8532), 128 Holland Park Avenue. *Good bar-luncheons and imaginative décor.*

Verbanella (229 9882 and 727 7282), 145 Notting Hill Gate.

ENTERTAINMENTS

Electric Cinema Club (727 4992), 191 Portobello Rd (C1). Shows an esoteric selection of underground movies and modern classics. Also specializes in Japanese films and other perennial choices of its membership (obtainable half an hour before entry). It is the second-oldest custom-built cinema in London.

The Westway Theatre (located underneath the motorway flyover where it crosses Portobello Rd). Free pop concerts (and occasionally experimental theatre) on most Saturday afternoons.

Mercury Theatre. 2 Ladbroke Road (727 7233). The home of the Rambert School of Ballet, and frequently open for public theatrical productions (check programme in daily papers).

The host of street musicians and buskers are described in Part One on pages 29 to 35.

E. Specialist stalls and shops

Some stallholders regularly change the emphasis of their stalls, and others prefer to move about the market. For this reason considerable care has been taken to limit the list below to those dealers who have not only done business from the same spot for some time, but who also have a long-established specialist preference. Markets change continuously, but while many new stallholders may qualify for inclusion, the majority on the list and maps (pages 124–9) will keep their place.

The guide has been compiled alphabetically according to subject. The reference printed in brackets after the dealer's address refers to his position on Portobello maps. Within each category dealers are listed in their order of arrangement on the Portobello, travelling northwards, i.e. away from Notting Hill.

The numbers of the stalls given in this guide are in most cases clearly marked on the stalls themselves; where no number is given in the guide this is because either the particular arcade is small enough to prevent confusion, or the stalls are not themselves numbered.

Arms and militaria

Street stall. Outside Alice's, 86 Portobello Rd. (F10) *Permanent display of army surplus helmets, gas-masks, berets, etc. Of little interest to specialist collectors (although their Norwegian Land Army fur hats appear on some of the most fashionable heads in London).*

The Stronghold. Stall 17, Westbourne Antique Arcade, 113 Portobello Rd. (D8) *Highly professional display of guns, daggers and all kinds of militaria.*

Stall 19, Westbourne Antique Arcade. (D8) Next door to The Stronghold. *These two stalls provide a powerful attraction for enthusiasts.*

Stall 8, Westbourne Antique Arcade. (D8)

Two stalls. 283 Westbourne Grove, Westbourne Antique Arcade. (D7) *One with a few knives and pistols, the other specializing with distinction in medals and militaria.*

Stall 28. Corner Portobello Antique Supermarket. (D7)

Stall. L. M. Minton Arcade. 296 Westbourne Grove. (C7)

Stall. Entrance 2, Portobello Antique Arcade. (C5)

Two stalls. Entrance 3, Portobello Antique Arcade. (C4) *Two adjacent stalls with the largest display on the market of guns and arms, uniforms and buttons. Highly professional.*

Stall 20, Harris's Arcade. (D3) *This stall combines all the best qualities of the market: long-standing connoisseurship, interesting and varied goods and charming and enthusiastic service.*

Art Nouveau/Art Deco

These specialists provide the visually most attractive group of stalls on the Portobello, for even the commercially produced goods always possess quality of style if not of technique.

Stall. Basement of M. and C. Telfer-Smollet, 88 Portobello Rd. (F9) *Always something of interest, with pottery masks a speciality.*

Stall 9a. Westbourne Antique Arcade, 113 Portobello Rd. (D8)

Stall 294. Westbourne Grove (C7)

Alexandra. Stall 20, Corner Portobello Antique Supermarket. (D6) *Specialist in 1920s jewellery, but handles all sorts of period delights, generally at very reasonable prices.*

Stall 10. Corner Portobello Antique Supermarket. (D6) *Large stock of Art Nouveau metal-ware of a commercial but pleasing kind.*

Collins. Stall 25, Shepherd's Antique Arcade. (C4) *One of the first Art Nouveau specialists to come to the market nearly ten years ago; still maintains a high standard.*

Stall. Upstairs, Shepherd's Antique Arcade. (C4) *Small selection of Clarice Cliff pottery on a busy general jewellery stall tucked in at the top of the stairs.*

Stall. Panton Gallery. (D3) *Interesting commercial 'Deco'.*

Stall 1. Red Lion. (D2) *Particularly pleasant service and attractive display.*

Nicholas Haywood. 198 Westbourne Grove. *Outstanding for lamps, lanterns, etc.*

The Façade. 196 Westbourne Grove. *Cane furniture, lamps, etc.*

Automata *see* Toys

Badges

No specialists, but the best hunting ground is by the Westway motorway flyover.

Beadwork

Stall. Entrance 1, Portobello Antique Arcade. (C5)

Belt buckles

Street stall. Outside Collectors Corner. (D4) *Devoted entirely to Tiffany brass belt buckles, of arguable age but amusing subjects.*

Biscuit and tobacco tins *see* Caskets, *also* Toys

Books

Stall. Opposite stall 25, Westbourne Antique Arcade, 113 Portobello Rd. (D8)

Stall. By stall 1a, Westbourne Antique Arcade. (D8)

Stall. 294 Westbourne Grove. (C7)

Stall. Back room, Portobello Antique Arcade. (C5)

Stall 8. Shepherd's Antique Arcade. (C4) *Attractive selection of late 19th- and early 20th-century children's books. Excellent value.*

Stall. Upstairs, Dolphin Antiques. (C4)

Stall 12. Red Lion. (C3)

Two stalls. Upstairs, Red Lion. (C3)

Bottles

Street stall. Outside Judy Fox, 81 Portobello Rd. (F10)

Stall 13a. Westbourne Antique Arcade, 113 Portobello Rd. (D8)

Brass, copper and pewter

Trad. 67 Portobello Rd. (G11) *All sorts of curious paraphernalia, including remnants from the ship-breaker's yard and other monumental decorative brasswork.*

Rod's Antiques. 79 Portobello Rd. (F 10) *Similar to Trad (above), but with greater emphasis on brass lamps.*

Street stall. Outside Alice's, 86 Portobello Rd. (F 10) *Good selection of brass door-handles, letter-boxes, knockers, etc.*

L. and M. Sutton. 91 Portobello Rd. (E 9) *A general dealer with a reasonable selection of brass and copper furnishings.*

Stall 33a. Westbourne Antique Arcade, 113 Portobello Rd. (D 8) *Small items of copper and brass.*

Street stall. On Portobello Rd, beside Corner Portobello Antique Supermarket. (E 7) *Pewter.*

Stall 29. Corner Portobello Antique Supermarket. (D 7) *Interesting old pewter.*

Stall 17. 284 Westbourne Grove. (D 7) *Copper.*

Stall. Entrance 4, Portobello Antique Arcade. (D 4) *Door brasses.*

Stall 16. Shepherd's Antique Arcade. (C 4) *Brass furnishings, etc.*

Stall 41. Dolphin Antiques. (D 3) *Brass and pewter.*

Stall 7. Collectors Corner. (D 4) *Excellent pewter and brass.*

Stall 28. Red Lion. (D 3) *Pewter.*

The Brass Shop. 23 Pembridge Rd.

Stall. Beneath Westway motorway flyover. *A large selection of door brasses and porcelain door-handles at the lowest prices on the market.*

Brass bedsteads

Alice's. 86 Portobello Rd. (F 10) *The cheapest brass bedsteads in London. Some are already cleaned and painted, but the best buys come from the stacks of untouched beds at the back of the shop, which despite their blackness clean up beautifully.*

Bronzes

No specialist dealers, but many of the general shops and stalls sell bronzes when they can find them.

Buttons

Stall. Entrance 3, Portobello Antique Arcade. (C 4) *Wide range of military buttons.*

Cameras *see* Photographs

Caskets, writing-boxes, biscuit tins, etc.

Street stall. Outside Jan's, 69 Portobello Rd. (F 11) *Extraordinary display of biscuit, tobacco, soap, and other tins (plus a few pot-lids). All in good condition and well worth close investigation.*

Two stalls. Back room of Portobello Antique Arcade. (C 5) *Large selection of brass-mounted mahogany writing-boxes, etc.*

Chess-sets

Stall. Panton Gallery. (D 3) *Specializes entirely in chess-sets of all ages and in all materials. Often accepts a challenge to play.*

Children's books *see* Books

Cigarette Cards

No specialists, but many of the stalls selling toys, books or postcards will have a few sets. No doubt specialist stalls will soon appear.

Clocks and watches

Stall. Weaver Arcade. (F 11) *High quality and therefore expensive.*

Stall 6. Westbourne Antique Arcade, 113 Portobello Rd. (D 8)

Stall 14a. Westbourne Antique Arcade. (D 8)

Stall. 283 Westbourne Grove, Westbourne Antique Arcade. (D 7)

Stall. W. Jones & Son, 291 Westbourne Grove. (D 8)

Three street stalls. On Portobello Rd beside Corner Portobello Antique Supermarket. (D 7)

Stall 41. Corner Portobello Antique Supermarket. (D 7)

Stall 1. 284 Westbourne Grove. (D 7)

Two stalls. 294 Westbourne Grove. (C 7)

Stall. Back room of Portobello Antique Arcade. (C 5) *Fine watches and jewellery.*

Stall. Entrance 1, Portobello Antique Arcade. (D 5)

Stall. Entrance 4, Portobello Antique Arcade. (C 4)

Stall 5. Shepherd's Antique Arcade. (D 4)

Stalls 32, 28 and 13. Harris's Arcade. (C3)
Stalls 18, 21 and 87. Red Lion. (C3)

Cloisonné enamel (Oriental) *see* Porcelain and Pottery, Oriental

Clothes
A large number of stalls and shops throughout the market sell both second-hand and new clothes. The most interesting are:
75 Portobello Rd. (F10) *Permanent modern boutique.*
Stall. Basement of M. and C. Telfer-Smollett, 88 Portobello Rd. (F10) *Good Victorian and Edwardian costume, and fur coats.*
Stall. Outside M. and C. Telfer-Smollett. (F10) *Floppy felt hats and tartan berets.*
The Good Fairy. Behind The Earl of Lonsdale pub. (E8) *Every Saturday a tent is raised in the back yard of the pub and a wide variety of jeans, shirts and army surplus coats and jackets are sold.*
Maudie Cutter. Stall, entrance 3, Portobello Antique Arcade. (D4) *Former actress enjoying selling her feather boas and fans. Delightful service.*
Sunset Boulevard. 306 Portobello Rd. At the Golborne Rd end of the market. *Dramatic examples of costume from the 1930s and 1940s.*

Coins and medals
(many of the arms and militaria dealers also handle medals)
Stall. Weaver Arcade. (F11)
Stall 19. Westbourne Antique Arcade, 113 Portobello Rd. (D8) *Good medals.*
Two stalls. 283 Westbourne Grove, Westbourne Antique Arcade. (D7)
Stall. L.M. Minton Arcade, 296 Westbourne Grove. (C7)
Stall 1. Shepherd's Antique Arcade. (D4)
Stalls 38 and 40. Dolphin Antiques. (D and C3)
Stall 20. Harris's Arcade. (D3) *Excellent medals.*
Stall 10. G. Portwine. (D2) *Experienced specialists in coins and medals.*

Copper *see* Brass

Crafts (Modern)
Throughout the market more and more modern craft stalls are appearing. The specialities include candles, silver, jewellery, Indian and African crafts. (Also at La Mode Nouvelle. 53 Pembridge Rd.)

Cutlery
Silver dealers stock silver and plated canteens and cutlery, but one stallholder only specializes in non-silver cutlery:
Stall 10. Shepherd's Antique Arcade. (C4) *An outstanding Portobello stallholder, who also sells in Bermondsey.*

Dolls *see* Toys

Drawings *see* Paintings, *and* Prints

Feathers and fans
Maudie Cutter. Stall, entrance 3, Portobello Antique Arcade. (D4) *Recalling her childhood on the stage by selling superb feather boas and fans (also at 1a Bassett Road, W.10.).*

Furniture and general antiques
Both the Portobello and neighbouring streets such as Westbourne Grove and Kensington Church Street abound in antique shops. Some of the most intriguing on the Portobello include:
Alice's. 86 Portobello Rd. (F10) *A quick turnover of Victorian furniture, including stripped pine and brass bedsteads.*
A.E. Barham & Son. 83 Portobello Rd. (F10) *Excellent all-round dealers, especially if you like the more extravagant products of the 19th century.*
Geoffrey Van. 107 Portobello Rd. (E8) *Fine and rare period furniture, sculpture, ivories and objets d'art. Father and son discover the most unusual objects with remarkable regularity. Most of their goods are esoteric and expensive, indeed theirs is the only shop on the Portobello which could take its place in the West End with immediate success.*
Porcupine. 258 Portobello Rd. *Specializes in stripped pine furniture (will also strip customer's own furniture to order at a reasonable price).*

Glass

Two stalls. Kensington Park Rd end of Roger's Antique Arcade. (E12) *Art glass specialist. (Wedgwood china is their companion speciality.)*
Stall 3a. Westbourne Antique Arcade, 113 Portobello Rd. (D8)
Stall 13. 284 Westbourne Grove. (D7)
Stall 5. Collectors Corner. (D4)
Stall 11. Dolphin Antiques. (C4)
Stall 10. Shepherd's Antique Arcade. (C4)

Glass paintings

Stall. L.-M. Minton Arcade, 296 Westbourne Grove. (C7)
Stall 22. Red Lion. (D3)

Goss china *see* Porcelain and Pottery (European)

Certain dealers in English porcelain and pottery tend to hold a few pieces regularly, but one could be lucky on almost any stall.

Indian, Middle and Far Eastern works of art

M. and C. Telfer-Smollett. 88 Portobello Rd. (F10)
Two stalls. W. Jones and Son, 291 Westbourne Grove. (D8)
Stall 86. Red Lion. (C3)
Stall 35. Red Lion. (C3) *Batik figures, and other East Indian works of art.*

Instruments (scientific and mechanical)

This wide category includes items ranging from genuine scientific instruments such as sextants to large mechanical objects such as ships' steam regulators.
Stall. Roger's Antique Arcade. (F12)
Stall. Basement of Roger's Antique Arcade. (E12)
Trad. 67 Portobello Rd. (G11) *Amusing large mechanical items.*
Rod's Antiques. 79 Portobello Rd. (F10) *Similar stock to Trad (above).*
Stall. Weaver Arcade. (F11)
Stall 22. Corner Portobello Antique Supermarket. (D7)
Stall 25. Dolphin Antiques. (C4)
Stall 31. Red Lion. (C3) *Always an attractive selection of small scientific instruments.*

Ivories *see Objets de vertu*

Jade *see Objets de vertu,* and Jewellery

Jewellery

More than half of the stalls on the Portobello handle jewellery so no attempt has been made either to list or mark them all. Those mentioned below are among the most specialized and/or individual:
Stalls. Roger's Antique Arcade. (F11)
Stalls. Weaver Arcade. (F11) *The many jewellers in this arcade are generally reliable and versatile.*
Stall. 283 Westbourne Grove, Westbourne Antique Arcade. (D8) *Some of the best jewellery on the market.*
Stall 27. Corner Portobello Antique Supermarket. (D7)
Stall 11. 284 Westbourne Grove. (D7) *Also does ring sizing.*
Jeff Borsack. Stall 7, 284 Westbourne Grove. (D7) *For non-connoisseurs the photographs of the stallholder entwined with the comedian Frankie Howerd are an attraction to rival the jewellery. Borsack himself is a professional comedian.*
Street stall. On Portobello Rd beside Corner Portobello Antique Supermarket. (D7)
Three stalls. Entrances 1, 3, and back room, Portobello Antique Arcade. (D4)
Street stall. Outside 151 Portobello Rd, Portobello Antique Arcade. (D4)
Stalls 21, 22 and upstairs. Shepherd's Antique Arcade. (D and C4)
Stalls 14 and 12. Dolphin Antiques. (C4)
Stall 12. Harris's Arcade. (C3)
Stall 5. Red Lion. (D3) *'Lil' was the first 'antique' stallholder inside the Red Lion when it opened in 1951.*
Stall 35. Red Lion. (C3)

Kersch collages (pictures composed of watch parts)

Stalls 1 and 20. Westbourne Antique Arcade, 113 Portobello Rd. (D8)
Stall. Panton Gallery. (D3)

Maps *see* Prints

Medals *see* Coins, and Arms and militaria

Medical
Stall 4. G. Portwine. (C2) *Specialist entirely
in 19th-century and early medical instruments.*

Metalwork *see* Brass

Militaria *see* Arms

Minerals
Street stall. Outside L. Guerra, 82 Portobello Rd. (G11)
Geoffrey Van. 15 Portobello Rd. *One of
their two secondary shops at the top of the
road.*
Stall 26. Red Lion. (D3)

Miniature and dolls' pieces (furniture,
ea-sets, boxes, etc.)
Again, items of this kind can be found on a
variety of different stalls and only the
principal specialists are listed below:
Stall. 109 Portobello Rd. (E8) *Carol Ann
Stanton has dolls' furniture and other miniature pieces among her dolls and toys (see also
her stalls at No. 1, The Galleries, Camden
Passage and in the Hypermarket, Kensington
High Street).*
Stall 55. Corner Portobello Antique Supermarket. (C6)
Stall 11. Collectors Corner. (D4) *An
absorbing stall packed with delicate miniature
items in all media including porcelain and
silver.*
Stalls 88, 37 and 30. Red Lion. (C/D3)
*Mostly Tunbridge, Scottish Souvenir and
other ware in the shape of small boxes.*

Miniatures and silhouettes *see* Paintings,
and *Objets de vertu*

Model Soldiers *see* Toys

Musical Boxes
Graham Webb. 93 Portobello Rd. (E9)

Netsuke *see Objets de vertu*

Newspapers
Stall. Basement, Roger's Antique Arcade.
(E12) *Pages from old newspapers hold
considerable collecting interest.*

Objets de vertu
Objets de vertu is a broad category covering
small collector's items normally executed in
precious metals and therefore of intrinsic
value. It is normally considered to include
enamels, snuff-boxes, European ivories,
caskets, some miniatures, étuis and other
instruments in gold and precious stones.
In this instance we have also included small
Oriental works of art such as ivory,
netsuke, jade, etc., as the same dealers on the
Portobello tend to handle both European
and Eastern *objets de vertu.* These stalls tend
to have an exciting but expensive selection.
Stall 9. Corner Portobello Antique Supermarket. (D6) *Specialist in netsuke.*
Stall 48. Corner Portobello Antique Super-
market. (D7)
Stall. Entrance 1, Portobello Antique
Arcade. (D5) *One of the longest-established
stalls on the market, handling Oriental
objects as well as European miniatures etc.*
Stalls 20 and 24. Dolphin Antiques. (D4)
Lucie Campbell. Stall 30, Harris's Arcade.
(C3) *A high standard of expertise. Generally
has some good enamel caskets.*
Stalls 14 and 1. Harris's Arcade. (C3)
Stall 5. G. Portwine. (C2)

Oriental art *see* Indian, Middle and Far
Eastern works of art, and *Objets de vertu*

**Paintings, watercolours, miniatures,
etc.**
Stall. Weaver Arcade. (F11)
Olaf Barnet. Collectors Gallery, above 89
Portobello Rd. (D9) *A mixture of modern
and contemporary paintings and prints, and
Barnet's own work. The painter's sense of
humour will disturb some while delighting
others.*
Stall 15. Westbourne Antique Arcade,
113 Portobello Rd. (D8)
Archer Gallery. 303 Westbourne Grove.
(C8)
Stall 48. Corner Portobello Antique Super-
market. (D7) *Excellent miniatures.*
Stall 15. Corner Portobello Antique Super-
market. (D6)
Stalls 27, 28 and 35. 284 Westbourne Grove.
(D7)

Stall. 294 Westbourne Grove. (D 8)

June Aylward. 115 Portobello Rd. (D 6) *Old Master paintings.*

Stall. Entrance 1, Portobello Antique Arcade. (C 4) *Miniatures and silhouettes only.*

Stall. Entrance 4, Portobello Antique Arcade. (C/D 5)

Street stall. Outside entrance 5 to Portobello Antique Arcade. (D 4) *Jean Carrau's amusing paintings on metal (plus lithographs). His eclectic style is a mixture of Surrealism and 1900s poster art.*

Stall 9. Shepherd's Antique Arcade. (C 4)

Stall 31. Dolphin Antiques. (C 4) *Outstanding drawings and watercolours.*

Stall. Panton Gallery. (C 3)

Stall 10. Red Lion. (C 2)

Stall 7. G. Portwine. (C 2)

Also see Caelt Gallery, 182 Westbourne Grove, *and several other significant galleries near by in Ledbury Rd.*

Papier mâché

Chip and Dale. 117 Portobello Rd. (D 6)

Stall 6. Nicholls Antique Supermarket, 142 Portobello Rd. (D 3)

Stall. Upstairs, Red Lion. (C 3)

Pewter *see* Brass

Photographs and cameras

Stall 88. Red Lion. (C 3) *Daguerrotypes, etc.*

Stall 72. Red Lion. (C 3) *One of the best camera specialists in London.*

Pipes and walking-sticks

Stall 44. Corner Portobello Antique Supermarket. (D 7)

Porcelain and pottery *see also* Art Nouveau/Art Deco

The majority of stalls on the Portobello handle porcelain and pottery in some form, and collectors of particular factories and types must find their own sources by experience. This list is in a sense a personal choice, and aims to give only those dealers with a virtually exclusive interest in porcelain and pottery.

1 European porcelain and pottery

Stalls. Kensington Park Rd end of Roger's

Antique Arcade. (E 12) *Specialist in Wedgwood (and Art Glass).*

Centaur Gallery. 82b Portobello Rd. (G 11) *Interesting ceramics among wide-ranging selection of objets d'art.*

Judy Fox. 81 Portobello Rd. (F 10) *A marvellous shop for those devoted to the late 19th and early 20th century. Mostly English Studio Pottery.*

Stall. Portobello Mews Market, Denbigh Mews. (F 10) *Generally has a few pieces of commemorative pottery.*

Stall. The Antique Arcade, 109 Portobello Rd. (C 8) *Blue and white transfer-printed wares.*

Commemorative Corner. Stall 13, Westbourne Antique Arcade, 113 Portobello Rd. (D 8) *A great variety of 18th- and 19th-century commemorative pottery.*

Stall 25. Westbourne Antique Arcade. (D 8) *An attractive stall of monumental turn-of-the-century pottery.*

Stalls 1a, 20a, 34a and many others. Westbourne Antique Arcade. (D 8)

Stall 18a. Westbourne Antique Arcade. (D 8) *Specializes exclusively in Doulton pottery.*

Stalls 8, 13 and others. Corner Portobello Antique Supermarket. (D 7 and 6)

Stalls. Entrances 1 and 3, Portobello Antique Arcade. (D 4 and 5)

Stall. Entrance 3, Portobello Antique Arcade. (D 4) *Specialists in Wedgwood exclusively.*

Stalls 3, 4, 5, 6 and 8. Collectors Corner. (D 4) *With such established experts as Betty Brandt and Alexander Raghinsky dealing from Collectors Corner this has become the centre of the market's porcelain and pottery dealing. Excellent Staffordshire wares and interesting Studio Pottery as well as the standard selection of 18th-century porcelain.*

Stall 37. Dolphin Antiques. (C/D 3)

Stall. Panton Gallery. (C/D 3) *Always attracts a professional crowd early in the morning. Fine variety of European and Oriental porcelain and objets de vertu.*

Stall 35. Harris's Arcade. (D 3)

Stall 23. Red Lion. (D 3)

Street stall. Outside Midland Bank, 148 Portobello Rd. (D2)

2 Oriental porcelain and pottery (including cloisonné enamels and other Oriental works of art)

Mr Satsuma. Stall 5, Westbourne Antique Arcade, 113 Portobello Rd. (D8) *Specializing exclusively in Japanese satsuma pottery.*

M. Goulden. 133 Portobello Rd. (D5)

Stalls 23 and 24. Shepherd's Antique Arcade. (D4)

Stalls 20 and 5. Dolphin Antiques. (D4)

Stall 22. Dolphin Antiques. (D4) *Cloisonné enamel.*

Stall. Upstairs in Dolphin Antiques. (C4) *Later blue and white porcelain.*

Two stalls. Panton Gallery. (C and D3) *A selection of high quality.*

Stalls 1 and 34. Harris's Arcade. (D3)

Stalls 1 and 2. Nicholls Antique Supermarket. (D3) *Excellent quality.*

Stalls 53 and 99. Red Lion. (C and D3)

Stall 52. Red Lion. (C3) *Oriental prints.*

Delehar. 146 Portobello Rd. (D3)

Postcards *see also* stalls specializing in Toys, or Books.

Stall. Entrance 3, Portobello Antique Arcade. (C4/5) *Also sells an unusual selection of letters.*

Stall. Upstairs at Dolphin Antiques. (C4)

The Three Hunters. Stall, G. Portwine. (C2)

Pottery *see* Porcelain and pottery

Prints and maps

Centaur Gallery. 82b Portobello Rd. (G11) *General dealers with a few unusual prints.*

Stall. Roger's Antique Arcade. (E12)

Stalls. Weaver Arcade. (E and F11) *Extensive selection of prints and maps.*

Stall. The Antique Arcade, 109 Portobello Rd. (D8)

Stall. Opposite No. 7, Westbourne Antique Arcade, 113 Portobello Rd. (D8)

Stall 23. Corner Portobello Antique Supermarket. (D7)

Stall 16. 284 Westbourne Grove. (D7) *An intriguing stall specializing in prints and watercolours concerning ships and the sea.*

Stall 44. 288 Westbourne Grove. (C6)

Stall 40. 288 Westbourne Grove. (C6) *Prints, books and watercolours about the South Seas.*

Stalls. Entrances 2 and 3, Portobello Antique Arcade. (C4 and 5)

Stall 30. Dolphin Antiques. (C4)

Stall. Panton Gallery. (C3)

Stall 15. Harris's Arcade. (C3)

Stall 52. Red Lion. (C3) *Japanese prints.*

Stall 9 and two stalls upstairs. Red Lion. (C2 and 3)

Records (discs and cylinders)

Stall. Upstairs at Dolphin Antiques. (C4) *Specializing in records of the 1920s.*

Rings and ring sizing *see* Jewellery

Scottish Souvenir ware *see* Miniature and dolls' pieces

Sheet music covers

No specialists on the road but dealers in books and prints frequently have some.

Silhouettes *see* Painting

Silver

Many stalls on the market handle silver and only the more specialized dealers are listed here and included on the maps.

Stalls. Beginning of Roger's Antique Arcade. (G and F11). *A number of stalls handling all kinds of silver.*

Portobello Silver Galleries. 82a Portobello Rd. (G10) *Vast selection.*

Stalls. Weaver Arcade. (F11) *Numerous stalls specializing in silver.*

J. Freeman. 85a Portobello Rd. (E10)

Stall 4. Westbourne Antique Arcade, 113 Portobello Rd. (D8)

Stall. 283 Westbourne Grove, Westbourne Antique Arcade. (D7)

Three street stalls. Westbourne Grove, outside Corner Portobello Antique Supermarket. (D7)

Stalls 38, 39 and 26. Corner Portobello Antique Supermarket. (D7)

Stall 10. 284 Westbourne Grove. (D7)

Street stall. On Portobello Rd, beside Corner Portobello Antique Supermarket. (D7)

Three street stalls. Outside and opposite
Casa Maria. (D 6)
A. Pash. 135 Portobello Rd. (D 5)
Stalls 10, 17, 18. Dolphin Antiques. (C 4)
Three street stalls. Outside Collectors
Corner. (D 4)
Three stalls. Harris's Arcade. (C 3)
Stalls 89, 76, 75, 27, 24, 20 and 13. Red Lion.
(C and D 3)
Delchar. 146 Portobello Rd. (D 3) *Experienced dealers.*

Snuff-boxes *see Objets de vertu*

Talking machines
No specialist stalls on the market to date,
but many of the general dealers handle the
occasional machine. (Graham Webb at
93 Portobello Rd specializes in disc and
cylinder musical boxes, and will also handle
polyphons, etc).

Taxidermy
Stall 20. 284 Westbourne Grove. (D 7)
*Many stalls and shops from time to time
handle stuffed bird groups under glass, but
this is the only stall to specialize completely
in stuffed birds and animals.*

Tiles *see* Porcelain and pottery (European)

Tins, Tobacco tins *see* Caskets, *also* Toys

Toys, dolls, automata, etc.
Graham Webb. 93 Portobello Rd. (E 9)
*Mr Webb is author of two useful books on
cylinder and disc musical boxes, and also
deals in strange and rare musical automata.*
Carol Ann Stanton. Stall, Antique Arcade.
(E 8) *The best-known London specialist in
dolls, also has toys, games, model soldiers
etc. (see also stalls in Camden Passage and
the Kensington Hypermarket).*
Stall. Antique Arcade. (E 8) *Specialist in
model and toy trains.*
Stall. Entrance 2, Portobello Antique
Arcade. (C 5)
Stalls 77 and 12. Red Lion. (C 3) *Model
soldiers, among other stock.*
The Three Hunters. Stall, G. Portwine.
(C 2) *A marvellous selection of Victorian*

*ephemera including toys, games, models,
postcards, etc.*
Dolls' Hospital. Bela Hajos Ltd, 27 Kensington Park Rd. (A 2)

Tunbridge ware *see* Miniature and doll's
pieces

Walking-sticks *see* Pipes

Watches *see* Clocks

Watercolours *see* Paintings, *and* Prints

Wedgwood *see* Porcelain and pottery
(European)

F. For prospective stallholders

The street market stalls for 'antiques' on
the Portobello and Golborne Roads belong
to the Borough of Kensington and are
delivered to their sites from 8 a.m. onwards.
There are no vacancies on the market at the
time of writing; applicants must join a
waiting list estimated at more than five
years (unless they can obtain an introduction to a legendary 'black market' in which
stalls are rumoured to change hands at over
£1,000). The weekly charge is currently
£1.87. Enquiries should be addressed to the
Senior Street Inspector at Hayden's Place
Sub-Depot, Hayden's Place, London W.11
(727 8114).
  Vacancies occur fairly frequently on the
Westway site which is run by the North
Kensington Amenity Trust, 3 Acklam
Road, London W.10 (969 7511).
  There are always vacant stalls in the
numerous indoor arcades which are marked
on the Portobello maps, although there is a
waiting list for the most popular pitches,
and for the older establishments it may
even be as long as for the outside stalls.
The price of an arcade stall ranges from
about £2.00 to about £6.00 per week. A
representative of the management is generally on the premises throughout Saturday
and should be contacted personally. Present traders are normally happy to advise
potential traders.

Portobello Road Area

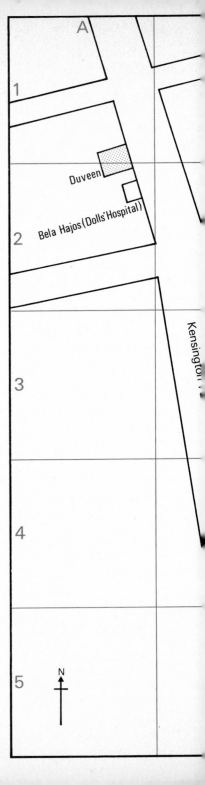

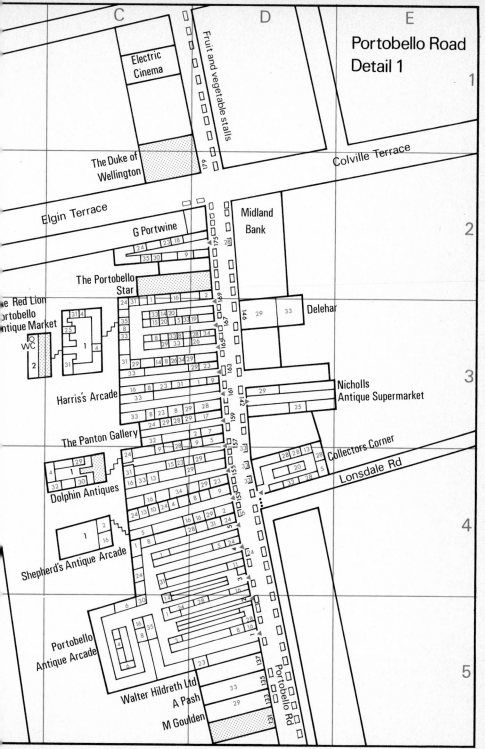

Portobello Road
Detail 1

C · D · E

Electric Cinema

Fruit and vegetable stalls

The Duke of Wellington

Colville Terrace

Elgin Terrace

G Portwine

Midland Bank

The Portobello Star

The Red Lion
Portobello
Antique Market

Delehar

WC

Harris's Arcade

Nicholls
Antique Supermarket

The Panton Gallery

Collectors Corner

Dolphin Antiques

Lonsdale Rd

Shepherd's Antique Arcade

Portobello
Antique Arcade

Portobello Rd

Walter Hildreth Ltd

A Pash

M Goulden

Continued on following page

KEY

1   Arms, militaria
2   Art Nouveau, Art Deco
3   Beadwork
4   Books
5   Brass, copper, pewter
6   Caskets, writing-boxes, biscuit tins
7   Chess-sets
8   Clocks, watches
9   Coins, medals
10 Cutlery
11 Feathers, fans
12 Furniture and general antiques
13 Glass
14 Indian, Middle and Far Eastern objects
15 Instruments
16 Jewellery
17 Kersch collages
18 Medical
19 Minerals
20 Miniature, dolls' pieces
21 Musical boxes
22 Newspapers
23 *Objets de vertu*
24 Paintings, watercolours, miniatures
25 Papier mâché
26 Photographs, cameras
27 Pipes, walking-sticks
28 Porcelain, pottery (European)
29 Porcelain, pottery (Oriental)
30 Postcards
31 Prints, maps
32 Records (discs and cylinders)
33 Silver
34 Taxidermy
35 Toys, dolls, automata
▨   Restaurants, pubs, snacks
▪   General stalls
▶   Entrances
B   Basement
G   Ground floor
1   First floor
117 Shop numbers

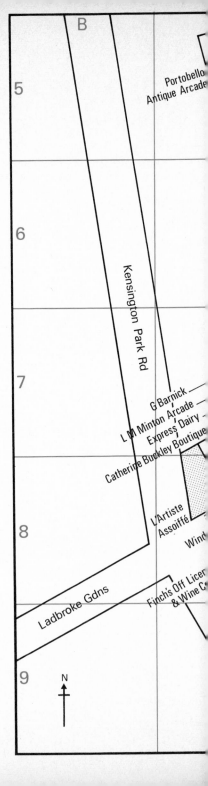

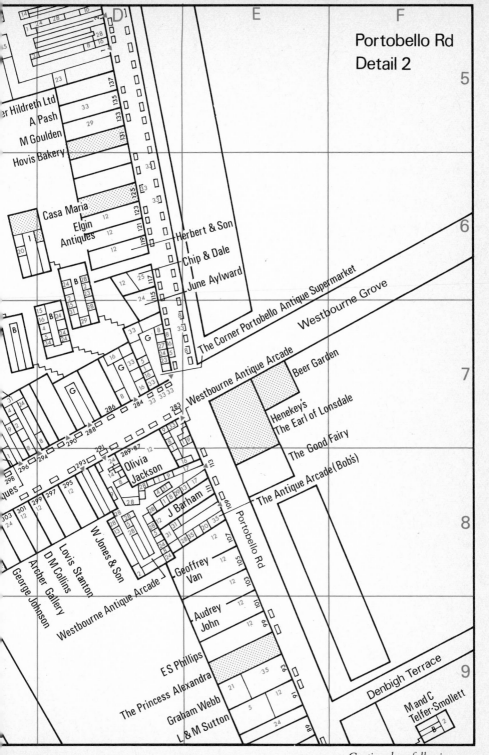

Continued on following page

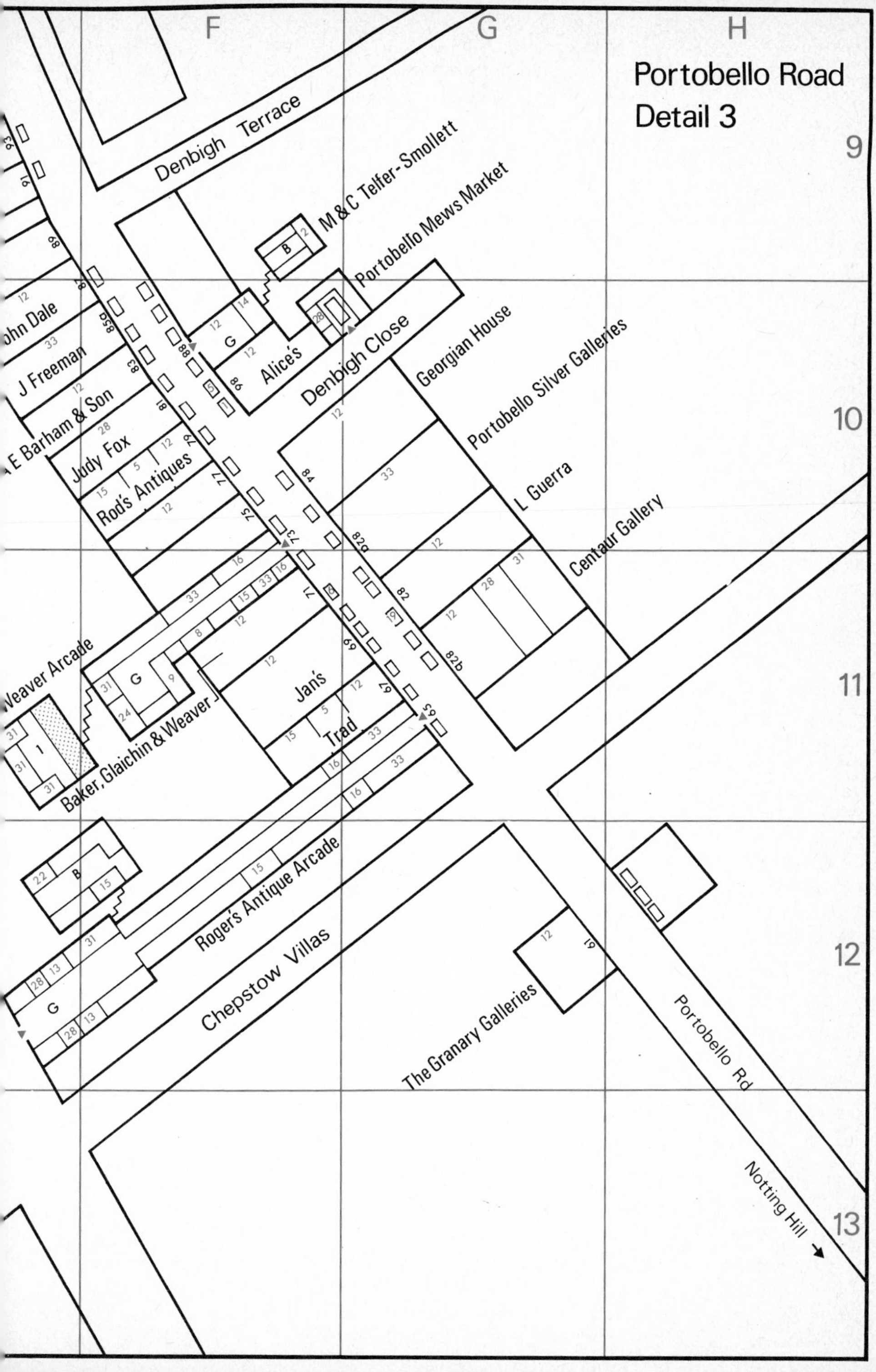

Denbigh Terrace

M & C Telfer-Smollett

Portobello Mews Market

8

John Dale

33

J Freeman

12

E Barham & Son

28

Judy Fox

15 12

Rod's Antiques

12

12 14

G

12

Alice's

Denbigh Close

12

Georgian House

Portobello Silver Galleries

10

L Guerra

Centaur Gallery

84

33

82a

12

28 31

82

82b

Weaver Arcade

31 G 9

24

33

15 33 16

8

12

Jan's

12

12

33

Baker, Glaichin & Weaver

31

1

31

31

16

15

Trad

12

33

16

11

22 B

15

Roger's Antique Arcade

15

Chepstow Villas

28 13 31

G

28 13

The Granary Galleries

12

Portobello Rd

12

Notting Hill

13

11 Bermondsey: The New Caledonian Market

A. Days and times of opening

The New Caledonian Market functions on FRIDAY (excluding Christmas Day). Official opening hours are from 7 a.m. to 6 p.m.

Trade on the open stalls actually begins as early as 5 a.m., and the heaviest trading is over before 8.30 a.m., even in winter. Furniture dealers arrive still earlier, generally soon after midnight, when business is done from vans parked around Bermondsey Square; but this exchange is strictly between dealers.

NOTE: Buyers should take note of an Appeal Court ruling of 26 March 1973 which stated that legal entitlement to goods purchased on an open market is to be secured by transaction only *during the hours of daylight*. In the winter months although the market is officially open at 7 a.m., it is still dark at this time and legal exchange cannot take place until later in the day. (This ruling only becomes relevant in the unlikely event of a market visitor inadvertently buying stolen goods. Previously the purchaser of goods in the licensed street markets kept his legal entitlement to goods whenever they were bought, provided he was not at the time aware that they were stolen.)

The New Caledonian is predominantly a dealers' market, hence the early hours of operation; but private buyers are made quite welcome and the majority of stallholders do not pack up their goods until about 1 p.m. Collectors should be warned that the open market is largely deserted in the afternoon (although habits are beginning to change in this respect).

The 'Bermondsey Antique Market', near by at 251–5 Long Lane, is a converted bacon factory, privately owned, which houses more than 150 stalls. This also functions on FRIDAY. Official opening hours are from 7 a.m. to 2 p.m.

Again, the doors open for traders earlier, at about 4.30 a.m.

The market owners, London Antique Dealers (407 2040), operate their own business throughout the week from this address.

'The Bermondsey Market Antique Centre', at 1 Bermondsey Square, contains a few stalls. It also opens on FRIDAY, times as 'Bermondsey Antique Market' above.

B. Range of items available, and prices, packers, carriers and shippers

The New Caledonian Market is the only street market devoted exclusively to antiques, i.e. without modern crafts, clothes, etc., and the range is wide, including furniture as well as ceramics, silver and other works of art. The largest body of material is naturally Victorian. Bermondsey has a generally high standard, and a reputation for producing with fair regularity objects of considerable historical interest. Since it is a dealers' market, prices are generally reasonable, and often low. However, the competition is fiercely professional and most of the good things change hands early in the morning.

Several firms offer a collection and delivery service from the New Caledonian Market. The collecting point for most of these carriers is by the pavement dividing the two sections of the Street Market. Reliable firms include:

Michael Davis (878 0102)
W. Wingate and Johnson (237 2628)
Bolton and Fairhead (734 6096)
Davies–Turner (730 3455)
Robert Fisher (734 6901) operates for collection from 1 Bermondsey Square, though the head office is in the West End.

C. Public transport (*see also* Bermondsey Area Map, p. 132)

UNDERGROUND: Borough Tube (Northern Line) is within an eight-minute walk down

Long Lane. Elephant and Castle (Bakerloo and Northern Lines) is within a fifteen-minute walk along the New Kent Road. London Bridge (Northern Line) and also London Bridge Main Line Railway Station are within a ten-minute walk down Bermondsey Street.

BUSES: (from north of the river) **12** stops within fifteen minutes' walk of the market at *Elephant and Castle*. From Harlesden *via* Marble Arch, Oxford Circus, Piccadilly Circus and Westminster Bridge (final destination Norwood Junction). **78** stops right at *Bermondsey Square*, the market. From Shoreditch *via* Liverpool Street and Tower Bridge (final destination Dulwich). **53** stops six minutes' walk from the market at the top of the *Old Kent Road*. From Camden Town *via* Great Portland Street, Oxford Circus, Trafalgar Square and Westminster Bridge (final destination Plumstead Common). **42** stops at *Bermondsey Square*, the market. From Aldgate *via* Tower Bridge (final destination Camberwell Green). **188** stops at *Bermondsey Square*. From Euston Station *via* Kingsway and Waterloo (final destination Greenwich Church). **18** stops ten minutes' walk from the market, at *London Bridge* (final destination). From Sudbury *via* Baker Street Station, King's Cross, Ludgate Circus and Southwark Bridge.

D. Food and drink

Breakfast being the principal meal at Bermondsey, gourmets must expect their food fried rather than flambé.

Two excellent cafés supply bacon, eggs, liver, kidneys, toast, tea, coffee, chocolate, etc. in any combination:
Rose Dining Rooms. 210 Bermondsey St.
Market Café. 124 Tower Bridge Rd.

STANDING-UP HOT DRINKS AND SNACKS:
Bill's van, parked on the Bermondsey Square side of the market from about 4 a.m. to about noon, serves hot-dogs, salad and cheese rolls, coffee, tea, etc., plus humorous chat and friendly abuse.

A snack counter in the Bermondsey Antique Market, 251–5 Long Lane, offers warmth and similar sustenance.

ALCOHOLIC REFRESHMENT:
The Hand and the Marigold pub on the corner of Bermondsey Street and Cluny Place is licensed to serve drinks from 7.30 a.m. on Fridays.

E. Specialist stalls

The quality of the market lies in its general trading, but regular visitors will find stallholders with specialist emphasis. However, trade is so brisk at Bermondsey that even stallholders with specialist tendencies will turn over a more varied stock than they would on the Portobello Road, for example. It is important to look on every stall.

F. For prospective stallholders

The 270 pitches on the New Caledonian Market are administered by the London Borough of Southwark (703 6311) and annual permits are issued for each pitch. The fee is currently only 70p per week, but there is a five-year waiting list. However the Inspectors at the market site are authorized to issue £1 temporary permits each Friday for trading on any stall that may be vacant on the day. These temporary permits are allocated according to the length of time the trader has been coming to the market, and regulars gradually work their way to the top of the waiting list for annual permits. The newcomer should talk to one of the uniformed Market Inspectors on Friday mornings, who will be able to deal with problems and requests on the spot. A space will almost always be found sometime during the morning.

The Bermondsey Antique Market at 251–5 Long Lane, S.E.1 (407 2040) operates more than 150 indoor stalls. The cost of a weekly lease varies, but is likely to be from £6 upwards. Application can be made to the management at any time, either in person on the premises or by telephone. Stalls fall vacant at frequent intervals.

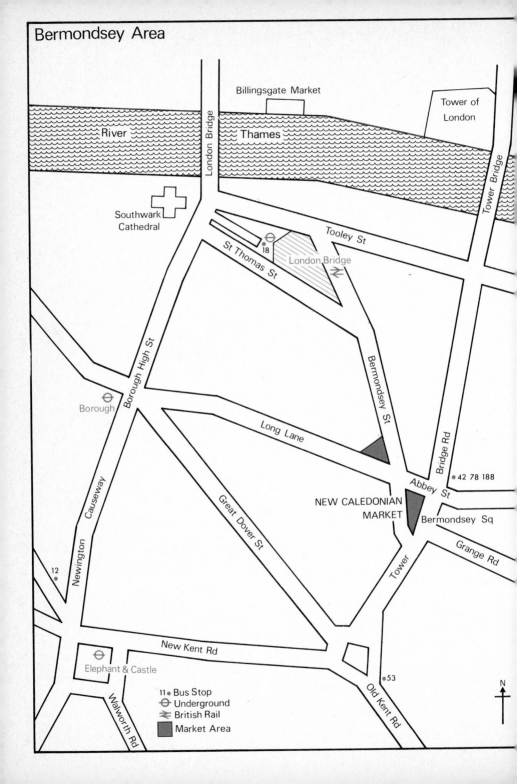

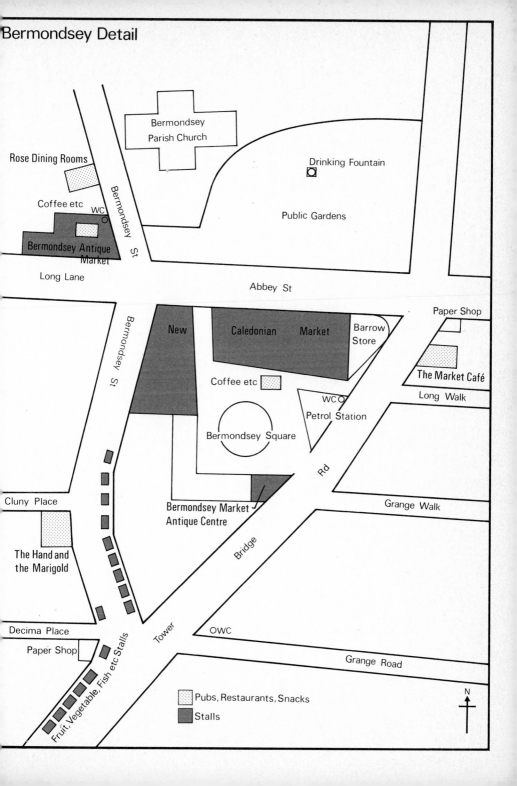

Bermondsey Detail

Rose Dining Rooms

Bermondsey Parish Church

Coffee etc

WC

Bermondsey St

Bermondsey Antique Market

Long Lane

Abbey St

Drinking Fountain

Public Gardens

Paper Shop

New

Caledonian Market

Barrow Store

Coffee etc

The Market Café

Long Walk

WC

Bermondsey St

Bermondsey Square

Petrol Station

Rd

Cluny Place

Grange Walk

The Hand and the Marigold

Bermondsey Market Antique Centre

Bridge

Decima Place

OWC

Paper Shop

Tower

Grange Road

Fruit, Vegetable, Fish etc Stalls

N

Pubs, Restaurants, Snacks

Stalls

12 Camden Passage

A. Days and times of opening

The principal market days at Camden Passage are SATURDAY and to a lesser extent WEDNESDAY. Opening hours are from 9 a.m. to 5 p.m.

In summer 1973 additional specialized markets were introduced, opening from 9 a.m. to 2 p.m., as follows: Monday, jewellery; Tuesday, furniture; Thursday, contemporary art; Friday, books. However these additional markets have yet to establish themselves on a worthwhile scale.

The shops and covered arcades in Camden Passage follow normal opening hours throughout the week and on Saturdays. As with most antique dealers, lunch hours and days off are taken irregularly, but visitors will find the majority of shops open on any visit.

There is a strong movement to allow both shops and stalls to function on Sundays as well, and if it succeeds this should prove popular. At the time of writing, however, only on Saturdays and Wednesdays are the stalls on the Charlton, Gallery and Pierrepont markets full, with a dozen or so more traders displaying their goods in the open passage running south from the Camden Head pub.

B. Range of items available, and prices

Although a number of well-known specialists have premises in Camden Passage, the principal delight of the market is the uniform quality of the numerous general dealers in furniture and works of art. Indeed the antique shops and small arcades are worth closer attention than the stalls. Prices are reasonable but seldom cheap.

The market stalls produce the usual selection of small collectable objects, together with an ample supply of cheap bric-a-brac. The average quality on the stalls is lower than in Bermondsey or Portobello.

C. Public transport   (*see also* Camden Passage Area Map, p. 137)

UNDERGROUND: The Angel (Northern Line) is the most convenient station. From the station the beginning of Camden Passage is a two-minute walk up Islington High Street.

BUSES: The following buses *all stop at the Angel*, two minutes' walk from the market: **19** from Tooting Bec *via* Sloane Square, Hyde Park Corner, Piccadilly Circus and Bloomsbury (final destination Finsbury Park). **30** from Roehampton *via* Fulham, South Kensington, Hyde Park Corner, Marble Arch, Baker Street and King's Cross (final destination Hackney Wick). **73** from Hammersmith *via* Kensington High Street, Marble Arch, Oxford Circus and King's Cross (final destination Stoke Newington). **38** from Victoria *via* Piccadilly Circus and Bloomsbury (final destination Walthamstow). Other buses stopping at the Angel which may be convenient for some visitors are **43, 104, 172, 279, 171, 277**.

D. Food and drink, local entertainment

The most fashionable and expensive restaurants in 'the Passage' are Carrier's at 2 Camden Passage (226 5353) and Frederick's at 106 Islington High Street (359 2888).

Aquilino's Bar at 31 Camden Passage (226 5454) and Portofino at 39 Camden Passage (226 0884) serve straightforward Italian food in pleasant surroundings, and are far cheaper than their exotic neighbours.

Rival coffee-bars are Natalie's in the Athenai Arcade and Terry's in the Flea Market, both of which provide excellent snacks at the counter.

Traditional café food is served at George's, 349 Upper Street, and The Sandwich Bar, 343 Upper Street.

Camden Passage also has one of the best-known pubs in London, the Camden Head, with genuine Late Victorian décor and for summer a forecourt with tables beneath sunshades.

Another source of provision is the Chapel Market off Liverpool Road, where the fruit and vegetables on the stalls are fresh and cheap.

ENTERTAINMENTS

The King's Head pub at 115 Upper Street (226 1916) has established itself as one of the leading lunchtime theatres in London, and the permanent company performing in a back room of the pub is supported by numerous visiting groups and artists. The lunchtime theatre is more experimental and less polished than the evening drama, but theatre enthusiasts will invariably enjoy the intimacy and enthusiasm of the performances.

Those visitors remaining in Islington for the evening can choose from two contrasting theatrical presentations, at Sadler's Wells, Rosebery Avenue (837 1672) and the Little Angel Marionette Theatre at 14 Dagmar Passage, Cross Street.

When the market succeeds in gaining a licence for Sunday trading, visitors should make their way at lunchtime down to the New Merlin's Caves in Margery Street, where George Melly and other jazz musicians give free concerts.

E. Specialist stalls and shops

One of the delights of Camden Passage is the quality of its general dealing, and the specialist dealers are far less numerous here than on the Portobello. However some shops and stalls do concentrate on certain fields, and these are listed below and indicated on the Camden Passage map (p. 139).

Dealers in each subject category are listed in the order they appear when the visitor is walking northwards from the Angel.

Arms and militaria
G. W. Traders (The American Shop). Opposite 104 Islington High Street.
Deane and Adams. 75 Upper Street.

Art Nouveau/Art Deco
Dan Klein. Stall 6, Athenai Arcade.
Chiu. 10 Charlton Place.

Clocks and watches
The Gateway Arcade. 355 Upper Street.
Nicholls Watches. 25 Camden Passage.
Strike One. Camden Walk.

Furniture and general antiques
Camden Passage is rich in dealers of standing who specialize in furniture and general antiques. Visitors will easily find them all along the Passage and they are clearly marked on the map. (A number are described in detail in Part One, pages 63 to 68.)

Instruments (Scientific)
Margaret Deighton. Opposite 102 Islington High Street.

Jewellery
Many of the stalls and shops handle jewellery but the two most notable specialists are:
Inheritance. 98 Islington High Street.
The Mineral Kingdom. 3 Pierrepont Arcade.

Paintings, watercolours, miniatures, etc.
Islington Antiques. 100 Islington High Street.
Roberts Antique Gallery. 347 Upper Street.

Papier mâché
The Corner Cupboard. Pierrepont Arcade.

Porcelain and pottery
European: Elaine Freedman. 108 Islington High Street.
Oriental: The Gateway Arcade. 355 Upper Street.

Prints and maps
Islington Antiques. 100 Islington High Street.
Finbar MacDonald. 17 Camden Passage.
Sports Design. 35 Essex Rd.

Records
D. J. Levey. 33 Camden Passage.

Silver
The Gateway Arcade. 355 Upper Street.
The Athenai Arcade. 354 Upper Street.
John Laurie. 352 Upper Street.

Toys
Jubilee. 10 Pierrepont Arcade.
Hinton Hunt Figures. 27 Camden Passage.
Carol Ann Station. 1 The Galleries.

F. For prospective stallholders

The open stalls on Camden Passage are almost all under the jurisdiction of John Friend, of Phelps Cottage, 357 Upper Street (359 0190). The stalls are situated, in order of desirability, at the Pierrepont Market, the Charlton Market, outside The Galleries and beside the Camden Head. Licences are issued to different traders for different days of the week, currently at £1·50 on weekdays and £2 on Saturdays. Mr Friend has been involved with the market in Camden Passage since the outset in 1960 and exercises his monopoly with considerable courtesy. New stallholders must show that both they and their goods conform to the standards of the Passage.

Prospective traders can also apply direct to the management of the Athenai Arcade (Mr Stanley at 226 5376) and the Flea Market (226 8211 and 226 6627) for the small indoor booths that become vacant with fair frequency.

At the time of writing new indoor markets are under construction at the Horseshoe Arcade opposite the Camden Head, at The Galleries at the northern end of the Passage and at 116–18 Islington High Street.

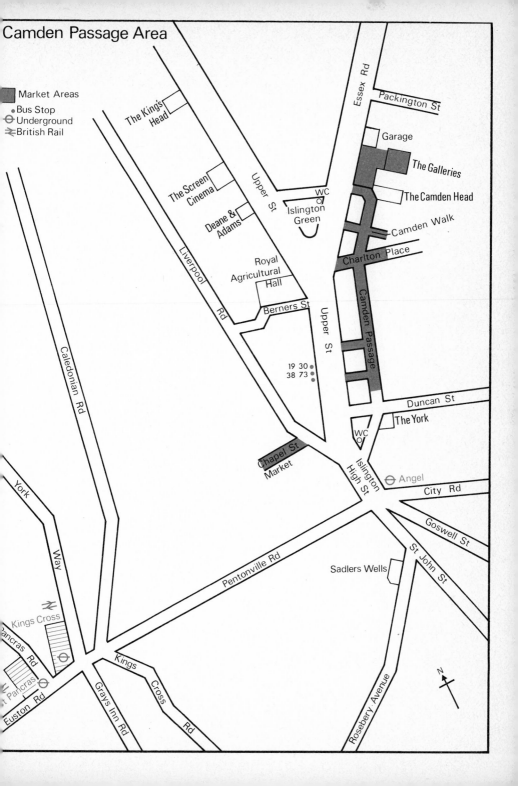

KEY

1 Arms, militaria
2 Art Nouveau, Art Deco
3 Beadwork
4 Books
5 Brass, copper, pewter
6 Caskets, writing-boxes, biscuit tins
7 Chess-sets
8 Clocks, watches
9 Coins, medals
10 Cutlery
11 Feathers, fans
12 Furniture and general antiques
13 Glass
14 Indian, Middle and Far Eastern objects
15 Instruments
16 Jewellery
17 Kersch collages
18 Medical
19 Minerals
20 Miniature, dolls' pieces
21 Musical boxes
22 Newspapers
23 *Objets de vertu*
24 Paintings, watercolours, miniatures
25 Papier mâché
26 Photographs, cameras
27 Pipes, walking-sticks
28 Porcelain, pottery (European)
29 Porcelain, pottery (Oriental)
30 Postcards
31 Prints, maps
32 Records (discs and cylinders)
33 Silver
34 Taxidermy
35 Toys, dolls, automata
▨ Restaurants, pubs, snacks
■ General stalls
▶ Entrances
B Basement
G Ground floor
1 First floor
117 Shop numbers

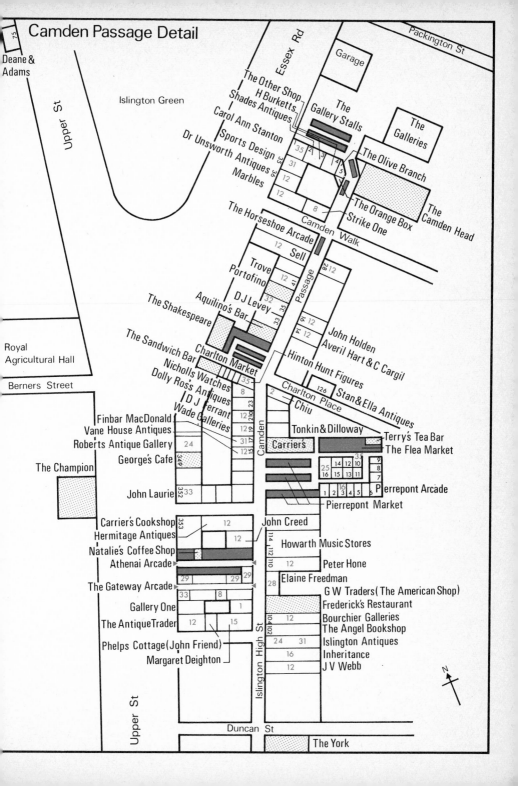

Camden Passage Detail

75

Deane & Adams

Upper St

Islington Green

Essex Rd

Packington St

Garage

The Gallery Stalls

The Galleries

The Other Shop
H Burketts
Shades Antiques
Carol Ann Stanton
Sports Design
Dr Unsworth Antiques
Marbles

35
31
12
12

The Olive Branch

The Orange Box
Strike One

8

The Camden Head

Camden Walk

The Horseshoe Arcade

12 Sell

Trove
Portofino
Aquilino's Bar
DJ Levey

12
32
33

41
35

28 12

Passage

John Holden
Averil Hart & C Cargil

Hinton Hunt Figures

The Shakespeare

The Sandwich Bar
Nicholls Watches
Dolly Ross Antiques
J D J Terrant
Wade Galleries

Charlton Market

35
8
12
31
12

Chiu

Charlton Place

126 Stan & Ella Antiques

Royal
Agricultural Hall

Berners Street

2

Tonkin & Dilloway
Carriers

Terry's Tea Bar
The Flea Market

Finbar MacDonald
Vane House Antiques
Roberts Antique Gallery
George's Cafe

John Laurie

24
349
352 33

Camden

25
16

14
15

12
13

10
11

3
16

9
8
7

1 2 3 4 5

Pierrepont Arcade

The Champion

Pierrepont Market

Carrier's Cookshop
Hermitage Antiques
Natalie's Coffee Shop
Athenai Arcade
The Gateway Arcade

353
12
12

29
33

29
8

29

John Creed

114 112 110

12

Howarth Music Stores

Peter Hone

Islington High St

Gallery One
The Antique Trader
Phelps Cottage (John Friend)
Margaret Deighton

1
12 15

28

Elaine Freedman

G W Traders (The American Shop)
Frederick's Restaurant
Bourchier Galleries
The Angel Bookshop
Islington Antiques
Inheritance
J V Webb

104 102
12
24 31
16
12

N

Upper St

Duncan St

The York

13 The East End Markets

Cutler Street Silver Market

A. Days and times of opening

The market functions on SUNDAY from about 8 a.m. to midday.

B. Range of items available, and prices

This is predominantly a dealers' market specializing in silver and jewellery, though a number of stalls sell coins, medals and even stamps. Occasionally a dealer may bring along some porcelain, bronzes and other items. Prices are generally fair, but it is not easy for the general public to secure the best silver against competition from dealers.

C. Public transport (see also East End Markets map)

UNDERGROUND: Liverpool Street (Circle, Central and Metropolitan Lines) and Aldgate (Circle and Metropolitan Lines) are the most convenient stations. From both stations there is a five-minute walk along Houndsditch to Cutler Street, which leads directly into the market in Exchange Buildings Yard.

BUSES: Sunday buses in London run less frequently than during the week, but the following stop near to Cutler Street: 78, 11, 15, 25, 9a (see details under 'From Cheshire Street to Petticoat Lane' below, p. 142).

Visitors will normally find it easier to approach by Underground.

D. Food and drink

The Baldacci Café, in Cutler Street itself, opens at 8 a.m., and witnesses a considerable amount of business in jewellery dealing, as well as breakfasting.

E. Specialist stalls

All the stalls specialize in either silver, jewellery, coins, medals or stamps.

F. For prospective stallholders

It is extremely difficult to secure a stall in this market and the best means of approach is through a present stallholder.

From Cheshire Street to Petticoat Lane

A. Days and times of opening

SUNDAY is the only day of full activity though some parts of the market do function daily during the week. Petticoat Lane market does not begin in earnest till after 9 a.m., but it is interesting to watch the stalls being set out from about 7.30 a.m. onwards. Cheshire Street, Bell Street and some others begin earlier than 9 a.m. They all continue until well into the afternoon.

B. Range of items available, and prices

At the eastern end of Cheshire Street there are many stalls and open market premises selling second-hand goods of every description, ranging from television sets, through saucepans to porcelain and glass. Every-

East End Markets

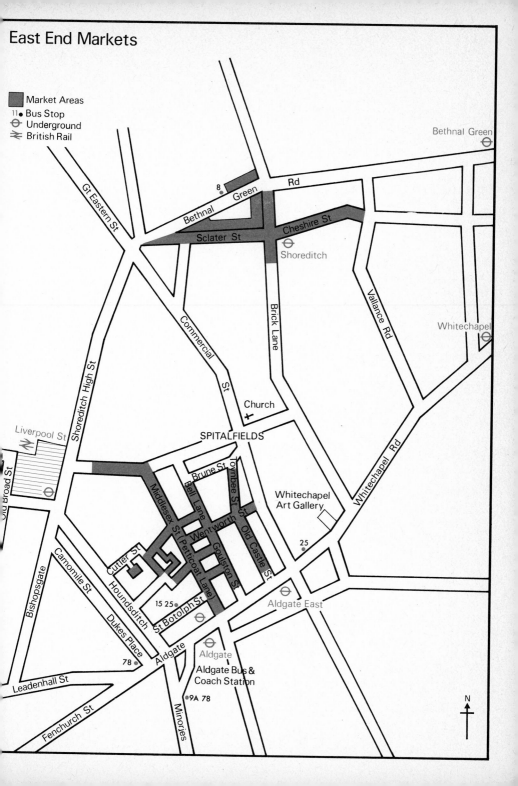

Market Areas

11● Bus Stop
Underground
British Rail

Bethnal Green

Gt Eastern St

8

Bethnal   Green   Rd

Sclater St

Cheshire St

Shoreditch

Vallance Rd

Whitechapel

Brick Lane

Commercial   St

Church

SPITALFIELDS

Shoreditch High St

Liverpool St

Old Broad St

Whitechapel Rd

Brune St

Toynbee St

Bell Lane

Middlesex St (Petticoat Lane)

Wentworth   St

Cutler St

Goulston St

Old Castle St

Whitechapel Art Gallery

25

15 25

St Botolph St

Aldgate East

Bishopsgate

Camomile St

Houndsditch

Dukes Place

Aldgate

Aldgate

78

Aldgate Bus & Coach Station

Leadenhall St

9A 78

Minories

Fenchurch St

N

thing is extremely cheap and collectors will often make startling discoveries.

Sclater Street, Petticoat Lane, Bell Street, and all the rest of the market stalls sell fresh and canned food, household goods, and other new goods at bargain prices.

The pet market in Club Row operates at its southern end, which is in effect part of Sclater Street. Puppies of all kinds, kittens, aviary birds, tropical fish, hamsters, pigeons, rabbits and other pets are on sale every Sunday.

C. Public transport (see also East End Markets map, p. 141)

UNDERGROUND: Whitechapel (Metropolitan and District Lines) or Bethnal Green (Central Line) are convenient for Cheshire Street, but the market is at least a ten-minute walk from either. The southern end of this market complex is served by Aldgate (Circle and Metropolitan Lines) and Aldgate East (District and Metropolitan Lines). Liverpool Street (Central, Circle and Metropolitan Lines) is convenient for Petticoat Lane.

BUSES: **8** stops two minutes' walk from Cheshire Street in *Bethnal Green Road*. From Willesden *via* Marble Arch, Oxford Circus, Bank and Liverpool Street (final destination Old Ford). **25** stops at the bottom of Petticoat Lane in *St Botolph Street*. From Victoria *via* Piccadilly Circus, Holborn and Bank (final destination Becontree Heath). **9a** (Sundays only) stops at *Aldgate* (final destination). From Mortlake *via* Hammersmith, Kensington, Hyde Park Corner, Piccadilly Circus and Aldwych. **78** stops at *Aldgate* (Minories). From Liverpool Street *via* Houndsditch (final destination Dulwich). **11** stops at *Liverpool Street* (final destination). From Shepherd's Bush *via* Hammersmith, Chelsea, Victoria and Trafalgar Square. **15** stops at the bottom of Petticoat Lane in *St Botolph Street*. From Kew Green *via* Ladbroke Grove, Paddington, Oxford Circus, Piccadilly Circus (final destination East Ham).

D. Food and drink, local entertainment

Many local cafés are open throughout Sunday and serve their normal fare.

One of the most popular Jewish restaurants in the whole of London is situated just round the corner from the southern end of Petticoat Lane, M. Bloom and Sons at 90 Whitechapel High Street (247 6001). This does a roaring trade on Sundays and booking is advised. (Take-away food is also served.)

ENTERTAINMENTS
There are two interesting museums in the vicinity, both open on Sundays and well worth a visit:

The Bethnal Green Museum, Cambridge Heath Road, is open on Sundays from 2 p.m. to 6 p.m. This houses the Victoria and Albert Museum Collection of dolls and toys, European 19th- and 20th-century furniture, and Rodin bronzes.

The Whitechapel Art Gallery, Whitechapel High Street, is open on Sundays from 2 p.m. to 5.30 p.m. The building itself is an outstanding example of Late Victorian 'aesthetic' design by Oscar Wilde's favourite architect, E. W. Godwin; the Gallery still fulfils its original function of encouraging local art, which is usually on display. The Gallery also mounts outstanding general exhibitions of 20th-century art.

E. Specialist stalls

Not applicable for this market.

F. For prospective stallholders

The East End markets are run exclusively by local traders and an outsider would have to work for some time in the community before being granted a Stepney Street Trading Licence.

However in Cheshire Street and some other areas of the market, anyone can set out second-hand goods on the pavement for sale.

14 The smaller markets

Church Street and Bell Street Markets, Lisson Grove

A. Days and times of opening

The markets in Church Street and Bell Street near by function on SATURDAY from 9 a.m. to 5 p.m.

B. Range of items available, and prices

The 'antique' section of the Church Street Market is located at the Lisson Grove end. (The rest of the street all the way to the Edgware Road sells food, clothing, canned foods, household goods, etc.) There are very few antique stalls and shops, but all are good value. The junk market at the Edgware Road end of Bell Street is also well worth inspecting (and see also Greer Books, a delightful second-hand bookshop at No. 87 Bell Street).

C. Public transport (see also Church Street and Bell Street map, p. 144)

UNDERGROUND: Edgware Road (Circle, District, Bakerloo and Metropolitan Lines) and Marylebone (Bakerloo Line) are within easy walking distance of Church Street and Bell Street.

BUSES: **16** stops in Edgware Road near *Church Street*. From Victoria *via* Hyde Park Corner and Marble Arch (final destination Neasden). **8** stops at *Church Street*. From Old Ford *via* Liverpool Street, Oxford Circus and Marble Arch (final destination Willesden). **6** stops in *Edgware Road* near Church Street. From Hackney Wick *via* Liverpool Street, Trafalgar Square, Oxford Circus and Marble Arch (final destination Kensal Rise).

D. Food and drink, local entertainment

The Church Street Market is close to the Marble Arch complex of eating-houses, pubs and cinemas, but the author has discovered nothing of note in the immediate vicinity.

E. Specialist stalls

Certain stalls do specialize (as in Victorian chairs or Oriental carpets), but these two markets are mainly general, and small enough for the visitors to find their way without listing stalls specifically.

F. For prospective stallholders

Permanent licences for street trading are issued by The Town Clerk, Westminster City Council, Westminster City Hall, London, S.W.1, but traders in Bell Street can merely set up stalls and pay on the day.

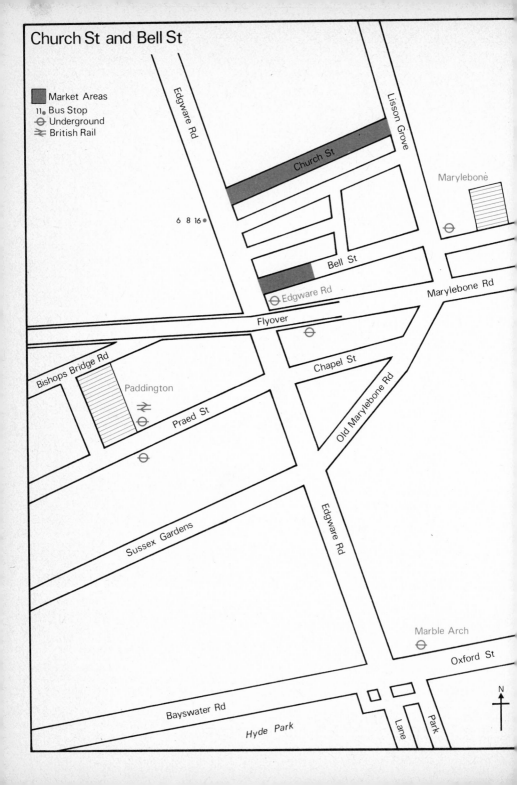